# THE LOWER SOUTH

IN

# AMERICAN HISTORY

BY

## WILLIAM GARROTT BROWN

LECTURER IN HISTORY AT HARVARD UNIVERSITY
FOR THE YEAR 1901-2

## GREENWOOD PRESS, PUBLISHERS
### NEW YORK

Originally published in 1902
by the Macmillan Co.

First Greenwood Printing 1969

Library of Congress Catalogue Card Number 69-13843

PRINTED IN UNITED STATES OF AMERICA

To My Brothers

WILSON RICHARD BROWN

EUGENE LEVERT BROWN

Who stood aside to let me pass

# PREFACE

THE substance of the first three papers in this volume has been given in the form of public lectures at Harvard University and at various Southern colleges. The three essays which follow are reprinted by the consent of the publishers of *The Atlantic Monthly*, and are but slightly changed from the form in which they appeared in that magazine. The other two papers have not been published before. No one but myself is responsible for any opinions or any errors, but I am indebted to many persons, North and South, for facts, for suggestions, and for criticism. The criticisms of Professor Guy Stevens Callender, of Bowdoin College, on the title essay, were particularly helpful.

There is something I might say by way of apology for the thin and fragmentary effect which the whole must have, but my impulse is to leave it unsaid, and to say, instead, what the slight hope is which I have in the book. The utmost it can accomplish is to sketch what now I cannot paint; to give an earnest of what waits on circumstance. For my true task, like many another task of many another man, must wait for better days : for days of confident mornings and calm evenings. Such his days and nights must be, and firm his will must be, his mind at peace, his silence undistracted, who would enter into the body of this civilization which I have tried to intimate with outlines, and make it live again through these and other of its times and seasons, he also living in it, and dying in it, and rising in it again. For that, and nothing less, is the demand it makes of its historian.

It will be something if these papers shall make it plain that my subject is a true body of human life, — a thing, and not a mass of facts, a topic in political science, an object lesson in large moralities. To know the thing itself should be our study; and the right study of it is thought and passion, not research alone. For this, like every other great and tragical human thing, passes forever into the mind and character and life of whosoever touches it, though he touch it never so lightly. If he himself be born of it, then he inherits all its past. It will forever strain him forth beyond his

narrow bounds of individual experience; darken
his doubt into bewilderment; insist upon its share
in his achievement; echo with its Appomatox his
little failures and surrenders. There is no other
such thing in the world. An eminent man of purpose, who will never condone a tragedy, called it
once "the saddest fact in all the world," — and
felt not, perhaps, how many dreary lives he compassed with his phrase.

And yet, it compensates sometimes, even while
it damns. I have come out of it and stood apart,
and it drew me back with a most potent charm.
Through and through it I have plunged, — from
end to end of it in history, from end to end of
it in physical dimension. Emerging on the other
side of it, I stood on the long hill by San An-
tonio, the low, gray cross of the Alamo beneath me,
where once in death it grimly triumphed, and
looked back upon it, and cursed it, and blessed the
flag of the Republic, fluttering there on Fort Sam
Houston, for a sign of the stronger and better thing
that overthrew it. Nevertheless, there also it persisted, conquerable but indestructible, stretching
thence back over the dark lands about the Gulf,
the Georgian hills, the Carolinian rice swamps, on
to the Potomac and the Virginian lowlands, where

the first acquiescence was, and the first ease, and
the first slow working out of sin.   And then — I
turned to the westward; and to me, as to Ober-
mann on his Alp, as to every man, greater or
less, who takes upon him the burden of a mystery too heavy for his weak heart, there came once
more, unsought, unreasoned, hateful, the old reaction and resurrection from despair.   Once more,
with eyes like theirs who from the Alamo looked
out upon the Spaniard, — like hers, the sweet-
voiced child's beside me, heiress, as I am heir, to
all the sorrow and all the tortured pride of it, —
once more, defiantly and gently, I faced the future,
charged with whatever repetitions, whatever fresh
bewilderments, over the Texan plains.

CAMBRIDGE,
    April 24, 1902.

# CONTENTS

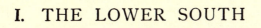

# I. THE LOWER SOUTH

# I

## THE LOWER SOUTH IN AMERICAN HISTORY

(1820–1860)

### THE RISE OF THE COTTON STATES

I WISH to discuss very broadly a certain quarter of the Union and the part it played in a certain period of American history; to describe a region commonly regarded as a sort of Nazareth, out of which only tasks and perplexities have come; to examine a civilization which many have looked upon as foreign to American ideas; to review a political enterprise which has often been condemned as contrary to American principles. My aim is neither to defend nor to arraign. I wish to inquire whether that civilization and that political enterprise were a natural outcome of material conditions and of what went before, not whether they were right or wrong. I wish to inquire whether the men and women of that time and region had the ordinary qualities of

3

human nature, not whether they were better or
worse than the men and women of other lands and
times.

The region I have in mind is the southernmost
part of the United States, and is oftenest desig-
nated nowadays as the Cotton States; formerly, it
was sometimes called the Cotton Kingdom.  The
period is the long period of material development,
of territorial expansion, and of domestic controversy, from the admission of Missouri in 1820 to
the secession of South Carolina in 1860.

Only two of the states included in this region,
South Carolina and Georgia, were of the original
thirteen.  The early history of the others, though
curious and interesting, is not much dwelt upon in
the formal histories of the United States.  One
learns from these that Spanish adventurers, the
immediate successors of Columbus, explored the
coasts of the Mexican Gulf; that De Leon was in
Florida; that De Soto made a cruel, heroic, bootless march from the Savannah to the Mississippi,
and was buried in the great river of the West;
that Mobile and New Orleans were settled by the
French.  One knows, of course, that the great
Louisiana Territory was bought from Napoleon in
1803, and one remembers rather vaguely that there

was a boundary controversy with Spain about West Florida, and that both the Floridas came finally to the United States in 1819. Then one ceases to think of the Gulf states except as a part of "the South." They are put into a group with the Carolinas and Virginia and Kentucky. If a particular Southern state is singled out for a representative, it is apt to be Virginia, as the oldest.

Yet the lower South differed materially from the upper South: not so much as Virginia differed from Massachusetts, but quite enough to make it necessary for us to distinguish between the two groups of Southern states. Let us begin, however, with a word or two about the differences between Virginia and the whole South, on the one hand, and Massachusetts and the whole North, on the other. It will be necessary to repeat some things which have often been said before, and it will not be necessary to controvert seriously the opinions maintained by recent writers of history.

The differences were not plainly racial. There were no race elements of any importance to be found in the Southern country which were not also represented in the East and North. The main stock, North and South, was, of course,

English, and it is not even true, speaking broadly, that Virginia and the Carolinas were peopled from one rank of English society and New England from another. To contrast the Puritan and the Cavalier, somewhat as Macaulay did in his brilliant essay on Milton, and to dramatize our long sectional controversy into a picturesque conflict between Virginian Ruperts and New England Cromwells, is a rhetorical opportunity which our occasional orators and our more literary historians have seldom foregone. That Massachusetts was settled mainly by preachers and tinkers is still a prevalent notion in the South, while the corresponding notion that the early Virginians were mainly cadets of noble houses is also still entertained, though of late years Eastern writers have often intimated that even distinguished Virginian families are sprung from indentured servants. Neither the Southern boast nor the Eastern sneer is justified by a careful investigation of the facts. President Tyler, of William and Mary College, the foremost of Virginian antiquaries, after long study of many genealogies, finds himself distinctly reassured as to the quality of early immigration. A fair judgment, perhaps, is that the nobility and the country gentry were represented in Virginia in about the same proportions as in Old England. But the English middle class, from which New England drew the mass of her colonial population, though to the southward also it was represented more fully than any other class, was not so well represented there as in New England. The truth seems to be that the top and the bottom of English society, and not the middle only, were drawn upon to people Virginia, while New England was stocked almost wholly from the middle parts. If one struck a balance, the two colonial groups were very nearly on a par in the matter of the English blood in them. The distinction which Virginia had in her upper class was balanced by the greater homogeneity of New England's population and the comparative unimportance there of the lowest class of Englishmen.

So, too, of the other race elements. The African, who from the first took his place below the lowest of the whites in Virginia, was found in colonial Massachusetts also, though there was never any great demand for him there, or any economic excuse for his presence there; and in both colonies he was a slave. French Huguenots, coming in considerable numbers to the

Carolinas, spread westward and southward. But there were French Huguenots in New England also, and the names of certain colonial worthies of that strain, albeit their original owners might not recognize them as we pronounce them nowadays, still designate many streets and public places of Boston and other New England cities. The Scotch-Irish, perhaps, in proportion to numbers, the most notable of all our race elements, particularly when one considers the leaders they have given to our legislatures and our armies, were strong in the western parts of Virginia and North Carolina, whence they helped to people Tennessee, and in fact they spread over the whole South, usually clinging together in small communities, to which they gave a character of industry and stability. But no one needs to be told how strong that element always was in New England, and particularly in New Hampshire, where many a colonial household went back for its heroic memories, not to any English battlefield, but to what was often called merely "the siege," meaning always the siege of Londonderry. Men shaped in the physical mould of Andrew Jackson and John C. Calhoun were to be met on many a village street in northern New England, as they were in the more thriving country towns of the South. Catholic Irish were, it is true, very scarce in Southern cities, and by the end of our period they were growing numerous in the North. In the closing years of the Civil War, their superb fighting qualities largely offset the waning fire and dash of the Confederates. Neither did the South get any large share of the continental emigrants who came in such a rapidly growing stream in the fifties. But a moment's reflection is enough to dispel altogether the notion that, except by increasing the population, the wealth, and the voting power of the North, the Catholic Irish and the Italians, Swedes, Germans, and other comparatively new race elements in the North had any important effect in heightening the differences between the sections before the Civil War. The only really important differences that had to do with race were the greater homogeneity of the English stock in New England, the greater mass of blacks in the South, and the larger proportion among the whites there both of such as had always been used to places of authority and of such as had always looked up to the authority of others.

Somewhat more important, but still not of the

first importance, were the differences in religious traditions and in those political ideas which are closely related to men's religious beliefs and practices. During the period of the Puritan Revolution in old England, New England was mainly for the rebels and for Cromwell, while the Southern colonies leaned to the side of the king. The victories of Cromwell drove many of the gentry to Virginia, and the restoration of the Stuarts led to an increase in the Puritan population of New England. The English church never had much strength there until comparatively recent years, while in Virginia, up to the time of the great Methodist movement, its ascendency was uncontested. Before the Revolution, how-ever, Methodists and Baptists and Presbyterians were already numerous in the South, and since the colonies became States no one of the Southern States has had a majority of the Episcopalian faith and form of worship. Nevertheless, that long remained the leading denomination among the upper classes of Southern society, and through its vestry plan of church government and its organization by parishes it had a strong influence on the social and political life of the people — far stronger and more important than any loyalist sentiment or any aristocratic notions about government which may have survived the Revolution. It contributed more to that divergence which gradually, in two centuries or thereabouts, from perfectly natural causes, and through no sudden or dramatic processes, made communities which began with the same political ideas unlike in their political no less than in their economic and social arrangements.

The economic and industrial differences were manifest early in the colonial period. In Virginia and the Carolinas, agriculture was always the main industry. The cereals were grown, but the chief and characteristic crops were tobacco in Virginia and North Carolina, rice and indigo, and to a less extent cotton, in South Carolina. The plantation system, instead of the small township groupings of New England, prevailed from the first, chiefly because good land was more plentiful and the chief crops could be grown more profitably on a large scale, but partly because, according to the prevalent system of church government, there was never any strong tendency in the people to gather about a meeting-house. In New England, each congregation was independent; the religious motive was, next to the primal physical needs, the strongest of all; and those of the people who lived by tilling the soil found that small holdings were most profitable. Negro labor not being adapted to the climate or the crops, and there being in New England no indentured white servants, large plantation establishments were never maintained. To gather in a comparatively thickly settled community about a meeting-house, to meet all together now and then in order to discuss the affairs of the town, to make the town the unit of political and military organization and the refuge from the Indians, — all this was as natural for the Congregationalists of New England as an entirely dissimilar arrangement was natural for the Episcopalians of Virginia and the Carolinas. A coast indented everywhere with estuaries, a fertile soil, a mild climate, a labor system based first on indentured whites and then increasingly on African slaves, invited the Southern colonists to disperse and take up large holdings. Their church system, with its parish and its vestry, made no difficulty.

The parish, comprising a reasonable number of plantations, became the unit of political organization. The vestry board, elective at first, but after 1662 empowered, in Virginia, to fill its own vacancies, did the thinking and the work of the parish, and there was no necessity for holding such assemblies as the town meeting, which would have been inconvenient for a people so scattered. On the other hand, the English county organization, which in New England never had any important part to play, was in Virginia a suitable device for such governmental work and such military organization as proved too big for the parish authorities and too little for the colonial authorities. The English sheriff and the English lieutenant thus reappeared in the New World with their functions and their importance rather increased than diminished. Such offices fell naturally into the hands of the larger landowners, who were apt to be, though they were not always, members of the colonial gentry. The county courts grew in importance, and the practice of letting the judges make recommendations to the colonial governor concerning vacancies in their ranks ended in making the county bench almost as close a corporation as the parish vestry. The New England town easily grew into a city. In colonial Virginia, cities would not grow of themselves, and legislation to make them grow was vain. On the South Carolina coast, where white men could not live on their plantations during certain seasons, Charleston grew into some importance, and so did Savannah, in Georgia; but plantations and small villages were in most quarters the only groupings of population. Even the court-houses at the county seats, though on court days they drew considerable gatherings, stood sometimes almost alone. Country stores supplied the immediate demand for merchandise, but as a rule the plantations got their supplies straight from England, the ships in many cases unloading at each plantation wharf. Commerce, seafaring, and manufactures, the sources of the wealth of New England, were practically unknown, save as conscious experiments.

The plantation system, as developed in Virginia and applied chiefly to the culture of tobacco, was sufficiently profitable to maintain the colony up to the Revolution. It resulted in a society made up of several layers or ranks. The slaves were at the bottom. A considerable bulk of impecunious whites, ill educated, lacking industry and initiative, getting their living mainly from the poorer soils, was next in rank above the negroes. A comparatively small body of white mechanics, tradesmen, and artisans held a doubtful place. Farmers with reasonable holdings and planters with great holdings, the two classes not clearly separated but on the contrary almost merged into one class, were dominant politically and industrially. With them were associated the members of the learned professions. The lawyers, in particular, were important members of society. It was a group of Virginian planters and lawyers who, after two hundred years of that life, proved by their work in Revolutionary times, and by their nobly rounded careers, that a slaveholding community, without commerce, without manufactures, without cities, without common schools, could yet produce men of the very highest wisdom and capacity for leadership.

It is well known, however, that these men themselves gravely questioned the soundness of the social organism from which they sprang. Jefferson bitterly lamented the fact of slavery, opposed the spread of it, placed the utmost emphasis on the value of New England's town meetings, and by destroying primogenitures aimed a blow directly at the plantation system. Washington's misgivings were as gloomy. By the beginning of the nineteenth century, it was clear that Virginia and the other states of the upper South, if left to themselves, would almost certainly change their

industrial system, and changes in their social and
political systems would naturally have followed.
As late as the beginning of the fourth decade of
the nineteenth century there still seemed a chance
that Jefferson's counsel would be heeded. Slavery in Virginia was a failure as compared with
free labor in the North: the profits of tobacco-
growing on the plantation plan did not begin to
make amends for the lack of those countless
material enterprises into which the people of
commonwealths but little farther north, whose climate and natural resources did not essentially
differ from Virginia's, had pressed with eager
energy.

When Monroe ceased to be President, and the
great Revolutionary group of Virginians passed
into history, there seemed little reason to doubt
that their power would fall into the hands of those
Western representatives of the New England
stock, already supreme in material achievement,
who in our own last half of the century held
so often the first places in the Republic. But
the sceptre, though it passed from Virginia, was
caught up by men of the Virginian strain. Not
even the men of the West, though they put forward Clay, who to a Western energy and West-

ern ideas added the old Virginian charm of personality, and though they soon learned to count upon the support of New England, which after the second Adams seldom had much direct leadership in national affairs — not even the growing West and the rich and prosperous East, combined or separate, could make headway against the new force which now appeared to battle for the institutions and the social organism, the material interests and the political ideas, which Virginia, falling backward to lower and lower rank among the states, with all the prestige of her ancient leadership and all the glory of her great names, was herself almost ready to abandon. As the power of Virginia declined, the power of the lower South rose. As the men of Virginia and the border states lost the first places in the national councils, the men of the Cotton states succeeded, not, indeed, to such preëminence as the Revolutionary Virginians had won, but to such a clear leadership of the South, and to such an ascendency in Congress and the courts, that for a quarter of a century they battled successfully with the men and the ideas of the East and West.

The earlier history of the Southwest, bitter as were the controversies which were provoked by the

expansion of the Republic in that direction, and voluminous as the literature of those controversies has
grown to be, still awaits the careful historical study
which has been given to the winning of the Northwest.  Even the picturesque and romantic period of
early exploration has suffered comparative neglect.
The Northwest has profited to the full by Park-
man's enthusiasm.  The explorers and builders of
French Canada, bootless as their work was, are
invested with a romantic charm in his pages.  All
of us have followed his soldiers, his priests, his
traders, in their heroic journeys over strange
plains, among the great lakes, up and down the
mysterious rivers, of the frozen land which they
sought to turn into a new empire for France.  The
red men of our imagination are the red men of the
North — the Hurons, the Chippewas, the Iroquois.

But how many of us have ever followed that
other and more promising effort to build up a
French empire in the lower, warmer, more fertile
region which the Spaniard had marched across
and then left to a century and a half of utter
darkness and mystery?  The splendid and bloody
pageant of De Soto's masterful expedition first
revealed to savages more powerful and warlike
than the Iroquois themselves the very existence of

civilization ; and his search for gold, vain as it was, first lifted for European eyes the veil which hid the most fruitful lands of the new world. When, after a century and a half, the veil was once more lifted, Spain, her Armada long since scattered and her imperial power declined to a second-rate importance, was falling backward in the Western race, and England and France were the chief competitors for the upper coasts of the gulf, the broad valleys of the Alabama and the Red River, and the still broader valley of the Mississippi. It was the young La Salle who stirred France to a sense of the greatness of the prize ; but how many of us who associate his name with Canada, the Lakes, and the narrow Mississippi of the Northwest remember that he himself meant to crown his life-work with nation-building on the great Mississippi of the Southwest, or that his ardent spirit passed away still farther to the southwestward, on the coast of Texas ? To his companion, Tonti, a figure only less attractive than La Salle's own, — to Tonti of the iron hand, and to the heroic sons of the house of Le Moyne, — D'Iberville, Bienville, Sauvolle, — La Salle's task was left. These names are unfamiliar, yet the work these men did has a more permanent importance in our own history

than the work of the Canadian pioneers.   A hundred and fifty years after De Soto, Spain still kept
a weak hold on Florida, but it was these energetic
Frenchmen who first planted civilization in the
Southwest.   Two hundred years ago they founded
Mobile, and a quarter of a century later, New
Orleans.   They placated the warlike Creeks, made
a firm alliance with the cunning Choctaws, and
fought two bloody wars with the Chickasaws,
whom De Soto had failed to conquer.   At the
mouth of the Mississippi they planted the civil
law and the Catholic faith so firmly that to this day
it is found convenient to keep on our supreme
bench at least one jurist familiar with that legal
system and preferably of that faith.   Their traders
and priests penetrated to the Red River country
on the west, and their easternmost fort was near
the present boundary of Georgia.   Alternately
waging petty wars and exchanging ornate courte-
sies with the Spaniards of Florida, they flourished
so under the unhealthy stimulus of John Law's
South Sea enterprise that the fear of the French
at Mobile was a motive additional to Oglethorpe's
philanthropic designs in the founding of Georgia.
But long before Georgia was founded unknown
white men — men of whom nothing is known but

that they were Englishmen — had penetrated the wilderness far to the westward of the Appalachian Mountains, and struck bargains with the Indians, and undersold the French traders under the very walls of their forts. Iberville had encountered an English ship in the Mississippi in 1699 and turned it back by a stratagem ; some thirty years later, when his brother, Bienville, fought his fiercest battle with the Chickasaws, in what is now northern Mississippi, he saw an English flag flying over their town. An obscure warfare of trade and religion was waged in that wild, flat region for more than half a century, until the long struggle for a continent ended on the Heights of Quebec. Then Mobile passed into the hands of the English, and New Orleans went to the Spaniards.

Georgia and the Carolinas laid claims to great slices of land extending westward from their proper bounds to the Mississippi, and farther south were the once Spanish, now English, provinces of East Florida and West Florida, which were loyalist during the Revolution, and so find no place in the histories of that second struggle for the continent. West Florida, extending from New Orleans eastward beyond Mobile, was, however, invaded and conquered during the war by Spaniards from Mexico, and both the Floridas came once again into the hands of Spain under the treaty of peace in 1783. Then came boundary controversies with Spain, and Spanish intrigues looking to the separation of the Southwest from the Union. By the end of the century the boundary between the Spanish Floridas and the United States had been fixed, the line running east and west from the Mississippi River to the Georgia line; and early in the nineteenth century Georgia, following the lead of the Carolinas, gave up her claim to the region north of the Floridas. Then Louisiana was bought, and it became only a question of time when the Spaniards would have to go. For a moment, Aaron Burr's mysterious enterprise seemed once more to threaten a separation of the Southwest from the Union. But our final struggle for the most disputed region in North America was with the British, who in the War of 1812 sent their strongest expedition to that quarter; with the Spaniards, who were really passive allies of England; and with the first claimants of all, the Indians. It was the men of the Southwest themselves who won the fight for the United States. Led by Andrew Jackson, they crushed the Creeks in the most obstinate of all our Indian wars, battered down the forts of Pensacola, defended Mobile, which General Wilkinson had already occupied, and at New Orleans won the single great land victory of the war. A few years later, Florida was again invaded in pursuit of the Seminoles, and Spain's protests ended with the treaty which gave us the whole Gulf coast from Key West to the Sabine.

But the lands thus won forever to English speech and English law were still for the most part a wilderness when the last century began. The Spaniards and the French had explored them for gold and precious stones, and failing in that quest had long confined themselves to trade with the Indians. They only gradually learned that the true value of the country was in its fertile soil, and they never gave much thought to its richest product. The English, coming later in small numbers to West Florida, and Americans, climbing over or journeying around the mountains, passed by the beds of coal and iron in the foothills of the Appalachian system and sought the lower agricultural lands. But the difficulty of separating the fibre from the seeds made the culture of cotton on a large scale

unprofitable, and the rice of South Carolina, the
sugar-cane of Louisiana, bade fair to prove the
main staples of the lower South until, in 1793,
Eli Whitney, a visitor at the plantation home of
General Nathaniel Greene, near Savannah, shut
himself up in a garret and set his Yankee brain
to work on a machine that grew into the cotton
gin.

In 1808, the foreign slave trade was forbidden.
Ten years later, while the Virginians, discour-
aged about agriculture and discontent with
slavery, were still pondering the words of Jefferson, thousands of English-speaking men and
women were sweeping over and around the
Appalachian wall, lighting up the forests, as a
contemporary declares, with twinkling camp-fires,
keeping pace with the march of free labor
across the continent to the northward, and bent
on growing cotton with slave labor on the lands
which Andrew Jackson had wrested from the
Creeks and defended against the British and
the Spaniards. Another stream moved down the
Mississippi Valley from Kentucky, Tennessee,
and other states to the northward. State after
state was erected to pair off with the new
states of the Northwest. Pushing in front of it

a fringe of moccasined pioneers, the tide passed on to the westward, across the Mississippi, across the Red River of the West, across the Sabine, until the Englishman and the Spaniard were face to face in the desert and the old affair of the Armada, the ancient quarrel of the Spanish Main and the Dutch lowlands, was renewed on the plains of Texas.

In the imperial domain thus slowly acquired and swiftly occupied were many material resources, many avenues to wealth that should have tempted enterprise. There were forests, rich deposits of iron and other minerals, a soil adapted to various crops, navigable streams for internal commerce, a reasonable number of ports for foreign commerce. Across the whole region, however, there stretched, from east to west, a band of dark, calcareous earth adapted as no other inland soil in the world is to the culture of cotton. This "Black Belt," varying in width from a score or more to a hundred or more of miles, and various fertile valleys north and south of it, at once attracted the richer and more energetic of the immigrants. The sandier and less fertile lowlands fell for the most part to comparatively small farmers, though their holdings

would never be called small in New England, for
each of them cultivated a dozen times as much
land as one finds in the farms of Rhode Island and
Connecticut. Such small farmers should never be
confounded with the so-called "poor whites," who
drifted into the pine barrens of the coast region or
built their rude cabins among the hills to the
northward. The great mass of the slaves belonged
to the men who took the Black Belt and the rich
valleys for their portion. The various classes of
Virginian and Carolinian society all found their
places in the new commonwealths, bringing with
them their political institutions, their religious and
social usages, their habits of thought and speech
and action. But there was a certain process of
selection about their coming, and then a sure effect
of environment and growth, which somewhat dif-
ferentiated the new society from the society which
had produced Washington and Jefferson. As a rule,
the emigrants were the men of the older seaboard
Southern states who were the readiest to better their
fortunes by changing their homes. As some one
has said of the English who came to America before
the Revolution, they were the men who had the
most "get up and get" about them. The same
process of selection continued as from Alabama

and Mississippi the more adventurous pressed on to Louisiana and Arkansas and Texas.

The form which Virginian society took in the lower South, the term comprehending South Carolina and Georgia on the east, and Louisiana and Arkansas and eastern Texas on the west, parts of Tennessee on the north, and also Florida, has been examined mainly from the outside, and usually under the guidance of general economic and moral theories. In the writings of Northern historians and political scientists, the moral weaknesses of slavery and the plantation system have been most emphasized. Mr. Cairnes, a very able economist of the school of John Stuart Mill, has surrounded the economic man with that environment and subjected him to such influences as could be mathematically reasoned out of the institutions which prevailed there, and particularly the institution of slavery. Mr. Frederick Law Olmsted, in his several volumes of travels, has supplied us with a mass of interesting, accurate, and intelligent observations. Foreign travellers have added much to our store. Yet it is quite possible that Mr. Cairnes's close reasoning, Mr. Olmsted's intelligent observation, and all similar attempts from outside, or at least from outsiders, have failed to

paint for us the true form and hue of that vanished
life.  We know that similar attempts of Europeans
to exhibit the true form and hue of our entire
American civilization by putting together many
minute observations, or by reasoning from a few
broad truths, have seldom succeeded.  We admit
the facts, perhaps, and we admire the reasoning,
but we do not recognize the picture.  A perfectly
faithful picture of the civilization of the lower
South would show at work there the forces and
tendencies which Mr. Cairnes discussed, but it
would show others also.   It would belie none of
Mr. Olmsted's observations, but it would correlate
them with other facts, not, perhaps, less important,
and throw upon them a light not quite so pitiless
and distorting.  It would, at least, enable us to
recognize those still existing parts and members
of the structure which time and war have indeed
changed and broken, but not yet altogether destroyed.  Surely, a true picture of Southern life
half a century ago should not seem altogether
strange to men and women, still living, who were
once a part of it.

Put in its briefest and barest form, the outside
view of that society is somewhat like this : —

The labor of slaves in the culture of cotton, rice,

and sugar-cane was profitable when employed on a large scale, and on rich lands, which, however, it soon exhausted, and so created a constant demand for fresh lands. Slave labor, however, was unavailable for manufactures, and far less profitable than free labor in the growing of small crops, because a slave has no incentive to thrift, care, honesty, and intelligence. It left no place for free labor of any manual sort, because it made such labor disgraceful. It tended to put wealth and power of all sorts into the hands of a small class, because small holdings were less profitable than large, and thus brought about the rule of an oligarchy of slaveholders, reducing the great mass of the whites to a state of indigence, ignorance, and listlessness. Mr. Cairnes describes them as "an idle and lawless rabble who live dispersed over vast plains in a condition little removed from absolute barbarism." This rabble, he says, numbered about five millions. The oligarchy of great planters, supreme at home, and wielding in national politics the power freely rendered up to them by millions of Southern poor whites and also the power they got through the Constitutional arrangement which gave them representation in Congress for three-fifths of their slaves, managed, by alliances with certain weak elements in Northern society, to dominate the government at Washington. They used their power cruelly at home, for contact with slaves bred contempt for the weak, and unscrupulously at Washington, aiming always to protect themselves in their peculiar rights of property and to secure, by breaking old agreements concerning territory already acquired, and by ruthless conquests of other territory, those fresh lands which slavery and the plantation system constantly demanded.

Every one of these forces was at work, every one of these tendencies was manifest, in the lower South. And yet, after some years of patient inquiry into the written and printed records of the civilization thus outlined, after following the history, from year to year, of a particular Southern state, after much free and intimate acquaintance with men and women of the old régime, after long study of the remnants of that already ancient and outworn vesture of decay still hanging in shreds and patches about the revivified South of to-day, I cannot recognize the picture as a true likeness of that which was.

For it was no economic man, no mere creature of desires and interests and inevitable mental

processes, on whom these forces played, in whom
these tendencies were at work. It was a Virginian but a few decades removed from Washington and Yorktown, from Jefferson and the
Declaration, from Madison and the Constitution,
from Mason and the Bill of Rights. It was
a Carolinian but one or two generations from
Marion and Routledge and the two Pinckneys.
It was an Englishman with centuries of the tradition of ordered liberty and slow progress in
his inmost thought, and in his veins the blood
which the Normans spilled for Duke William
when he brought to England the rudimentary
forms of jury justice and the blood which the
Saxon spilled for King Harold when he fought
with Duke William for England's right to name
her own rulers. It was a Scotch-Irishman whose
ancestors had lived through the siege of 'Derry
and given to the northern parts of Ireland the
prosperity so little shared by its southern parts.
It was a French Huguenot of the strain of them
that followed Henry of Navarre to the throne
and Coligny to the block. And so, too, of the
slave from whose abasement it is so easy to infer
the degeneracy of the master and the degrada-
tion of all who were neither masters nor slaves.

He was no mere black impersonation of those
qualities alone which servitude implies. He was
an individual with his individual peculiarities and
of a race with marked characteristics of its own.
Naturally without the progressive impulses of
his master, he was at once less sensitive than
his master would have been to the horrors and
the shame of servitude, and capable, as his master would never have been, of fealty and affection
to the very hand that chained him. He could
find some incentive to industry in the difference
between the lot he might have if he were a
house servant and the lot he would have as a
field hand. Slavery was, in the well-known
phrase of Clay, " a curse to the master and a
wrong to the slave." But it was not an unmiti-
gated wrong to the slave; and two centuries of
it in Virginia and half a century of it in the
Black Belt were not enough to destroy the moral
fibre of the master, to cheat him of his racial
birthright, or to ban him from the portals of
modern civilization.

I wish to sketch, as simply as I can, in outline,
but faithfully, the form which slavery and the
plantation system took during their new lease of
life after the occupation of the lower South,

in the particular Southern commonwealth with whose history I am most familiar. As it happens, it is perhaps the best of the Cotton states to use for an example, by reason of its central geographical position and the typicalness of its population and its civilization.

In 1850, when Alabama had been thirty years a state, her population was about three-quarters of a million, and the proportion of slaves to freemen was about three to four. The total included a small percentage of Catholic French, partly made up of the descendants of the French who settled Mobile, partly of more recent colonists, veterans of the Napoleonic wars, who had first built up a community of their own in a county which they named for the battle of Marengo and then scattered and intermarried with people of English descent. This French element, more interesting than important, and a similarly unimportant Spanish element, both confined for the most part to points near the Gulf coast, were the only race elements in the Cotton states that were not found in Virginia and the Carolinas.

Like Virginia, Alabama was in 1850 a distinctly agricultural community. What industrial difference there was did not lie in any greater diversification of industries but in the somewhat changed character of the main industry as it was practised in the younger commonwealth. The growing of cotton gave to slave labor its best opportunity : the cotton planter profited most by that one quality in which, according to Mr. Cairnes, slave labor excels — its capacity for organization and combination. As a rule, the large slave owners of Alabama were either cotton planters or members of the learned professions, who lived in the towns, and the great mass of the slaves belonged to a comparatively small number of men. As a matter of fact, less than thirty thousand persons, that is to say, less than seven per cent of the white population of Alabama, owned the three hundred and thirty-five thousand slaves in the state. The average holding of slaves was therefore between eleven and twelve. Three-fourths of all the slaves were owned by less than ten thousand men.

The land holdings of these men were in proportion to their holdings of slaves. Their plantations frequently included thousands of acres, and from the big plantations came the bulk of the cotton crop. Its average annual value was about 20 millions of dollars. There were only twelve small cotton factories in the state, so that practically all of the product was sent to New England or exported to Europe. The total annual exports of the state, cotton, of course, being the chief, were $10\frac{1}{2}$ millions; the imports, less than one million. Alabama therefore contributed, as did all the Cotton states, far more than her share to the country's favorable balance of trade; and it should be added that her product contributed materially to the prosperity of other sections. Yancey, the Alabamian orator, visiting New England and observing the stony and unfruitful soil, was at a loss to explain the wealth of the East until he saw cotton bales on the wharves at Boston and visited the cotton mills of neighboring cities. No doubt, he exaggerated the importance of what he saw; but the East certainly profited by the Southern market. The new Northwestern states were even more deeply indebted to the lower South than the East was; their prosperity may in fact be dated from the development of a region which did not raise its own bread and meat, and which could be reached by rivers that had their sources near the Great Lakes and their mouths on the Gulf. The Cotton states first offered to the West, before the building of east and west railroads, a market for those cereal crops which now make the upper Mississippi Valley the granary of the world.

For even those Alabama farmers who owned but one or two slaves, or no slaves at all, were nevertheless devoted in their loyalty to King Cotton. They seldom grew more corn and potatoes, or any other of the many food products for which their land was fit, or bred more cattle and swine, than they required for their own use; frequently, they did not raise enough food for their own use. The supreme attractiveness of cotton was due to the readiness with which it could be turned into money, the simplicity of the methods by which it was grown, and the comparative ease with which it could be marketed, even in a country of bad roads, which had as yet less than two hundred miles of railroads. The steamboats, plying all the navigable rivers, enlivening the forests with their steam calliopes, and brightening the lowlands at night with their brilliant cabin lights, were the chief representatives of modern methods of transportation. Cotton was hauled from the plantation to the nearest river bluff, the bales went sliding down an incline to the waiting steamboat, and so passed on to Mobile, New Orleans, Boston,

Liverpool. The planter perhaps followed his crop as far as Mobile or New Orleans, made a settlement with his agent, enjoyed his annual outing, and returned with his supplies for another year, not neglecting a proper provision for the fortnight's feasting and jollity at the approaching Christmastide.

That was the industrial life of the farmers and planters, who with their dependents and slaves made up more than half the entire population of the state. It differed from the industrial life of the same classes in Virginia chiefly in the concentration of land and slaves in fewer hands, in the greater immediate profitableness of agriculture, and in the greater rapidity with which lands were exhausted. Manufactures, banking, commerce, and all other industries to which the term "business" is ordinarily applied, can scarcely have supported more than seventy-five thousand or one hundred thousand white persons, employing perhaps as many negro slaves. As in Virginia, there were no great cities; in fact, Mobile alone had any good claim to be called a city. But small towns sprang up somewhat rapidly, partly because the separate plantations could not be reached by water so easily as in Virginia, partly

because the parish system of church government
had no effect on the grouping of the population,
and partly, perhaps, because the greater loneliness
of plantation life drew people together. Of the
parish, in fact, one hears almost nothing in the
lower South, except in Louisiana; and the parishes
there, of a different origin, and bearing French
names, corresponded to the counties, not the
parishes, of Virginia.

The Southern country town, eclipsed by the
more picturesque plantation, has been somewhat
neglected in literature; yet it also had its charm
and its importance. It could not do the work of
a city; it was quite unlike a New England village;
it was not much like a Western town. Its leading
citizens were planters, each of whom had at least
one plantation, and not rarely several, in the
county, half a dozen lawyers and politicians, the
ministers of several churches, one or two physi-
cians, and perhaps the teaching staff of a college
or seminary. Two or three general stores, a livery
stable, a bank, and the county court-house fronted
on the principal square or were ranged along the
main thoroughfare. There might be a small grog-
shop in some inconspicuous place; but there was
a strong feeling in many such small communities

in favor of prohibition on the local option plan. The houses of the planters and professional men, usually in the outskirts of the town, were spacious, as a rule, and had frequently some claim to elegance. On Saturdays, the stores were crowded with small farmers and negroes from the surrounding country, and during court week and in Christmas time one might see perhaps a thousand people and many vehicles. Ordinarily, and particularly in summer time, the whole aspect of such a community was one of almost dreamy idleness.

There remains one other sort of industrial life; but the word "industrial" is too much like industrious to be safely applied to it. The people of the hills and the sand barrens, the true "poor whites," need no lengthy description. The class still exists, practically unchanged, for these people had no part in slavery and the plantation system, and it is hard to find any betterment of their state from the overthrow of slavery. Many of them, living in the mountainous regions, content to win a bare subsistence from the unfruitful surface of the hills which held in their bowels the immense mineral wealth of the state, never saw a negro from year to year, and never came in contact with the planters of the Black Belt and

the river valleys until they, stripped of their
wealth and slaves by the war, turned from their
exhausted fields to the hills they had so long
neglected, and disturbed, with their railroads and
their furnaces, the remote, unthrifty, unambitious,
inscrutable people of the squalid cabin and the
long rifle and the chin beard and the hidden distil-
lery and the oddly Elizabethan speech, who for
three hundred years have not even noted the
growth of America or the progress of the world.
In the industrial life, the intellectual life, the
political life, and the actively religious life of the
South, these people had no part under slavery,
and they have none under freedom. If it was
they whom Mr. Cairnes meant when he spoke of
an " idle and lawless rabble," — and I can find
nowhere else Alabama's share of the five millions
of such people whom he credits to the whole
South, — it is difficult to accept his theory that
slavery alone produced them, since under freedom
they have not changed or disappeared.

Among the white people of Alabama who did
play a part in its history there was an intense
religious life, a limited, but not entirely arrested,
intellectual development, and a political activity
far more notable than any to be found under the

peculiar conditions, resulting from the Civil War and from Reconstruction, which now prevail.

The various Protestant denominations, particularly the Baptists and Methodists, were strong everywhere, the main strength of the Episcopalians being among the richer planters and their associates. There were nearly fifteen hundred houses of worship; the traveller was apt to find one wherever two highways crossed. Here the people gathered every Sunday and listened, with reverence and implicit faith, to a long sermon, usually rhetorical in its style and orthodox in its teaching. Unitarianism, Universalism, and similar religious movements of a progressive or revolutionary tendency never spread into the South, where the churches always exercised a distinctly conservative influence on thought in general. After the service at a country meeting-house, there was a half hour of gossip about crops, the weather, and politics. Then the people went home to their midday dinner: the wealthy in fine carriages, others in wagons or on horses and mules. Camp meetings were an early and natural device among so scattered a people. They were sometimes immense gatherings, arousing the utmost fervor.

Schools did not multiply like churches. There was no organized public school system until the end of the fifties. But about a thousand public schools, maintained chiefly from gifts of the general government, offered rudimentary instruction to less than thirty thousand children. There were, however, some really good academies attended by the children of the comparatively well-to-do, and there were several colleges which compared quite favorably with similar institutions in the West, and even with the smaller colleges of the older eastern communities. A surprising progress had been made in the development of girls' colleges. The percentage of illiterates was large, but this was chiefly due to the people of the hills and the pine barrens. Tutors were commonly employed on the great plantations, and the sons of such households were frequently sent to Eastern colleges and trained for learned professions.

There were many men and women who cared about books, and some private libraries well stocked with Greek and Latin and English classics; but there was little interest in contemporary literature, and no important literary activity. Only one person confessed to the census taker in 1850 that authorship was his (or perhaps her) occupation, though four or five Alabamians wrote books with some skill in composition and won some favor with the public. Practically all the planter's books, and everything else he read except his weekly political and religious newspapers, came, like his tools and furniture, from the North, or from England, or, if he lived near New Orleans, from France. Even his children's school books came, along with their tutor or governess, from New England or old England. Sargent S. Prentiss and William H. Seward are examples of New England tutors; Philip Henry Gosse, the naturalist, brother to Edmund Gosse, the man of letters, was an English tutor in the household of an Alabamian planter.

The best intellect of the state went sometimes into the ministry or into medicine, but oftener into the law, and through the law into politics, though the proportion of highly endowed young men who sought careers in the small army and navy of those days was probably larger than in the East or the West, where young men of like endowments and temper of mind were attracted by great business enterprises. As to the bar, one would think that the want of great cities and of great industrial enterprises might have put lawyers at a disadvantage as compared with their brethren of the North. But whether able men turned to the law because there were few other openings, or because, among a people who cared more for oratory than for any other art, the law was the surest avenue to distinction, to the law they did turn most frequently. One result was that in Alabama the courts, notwithstanding it became the custom to elect judges instead of appointing them, early attained and long maintained a high standard of excellence. The decisions of the Supreme Court took high rank with lawyers and law writers everywhere.

Internally, the state was in the main well governed, according to the Jeffersonian idea of government. There was no such predominance of the great planter class as one might expect. Governors and legislators were chosen from various social ranks; many prominent men were distinctly of the self-made type. The state had its period of folly over banks and paper money, but the opposition to the experiment was ably led, and when the costly lesson had been learned the people and their representatives paid for their folly manfully, frowning down the

least suggestion of repudiation, and even over-
throwing the party in power to get a sound
governor elected. The part which the men of
Alabama and the other Cotton states played in
Federal politics, and the long fight they made for
national ascendency, is another matter, and our
proper subject.

But before we turn to the militant aspect of
that civilization, I wish to say one word more of
its inner quality. Before we take our view of the
men of the lower South framing laws in Congress,
carrying out their policies in the Cabinet and
the White House, or making ready for battlefields, let us glance at them once more in their
homes, planting their fields, enjoying their chief
diversions of riding and hunting, celebrating
their feasts, solemnizing their marriages, burying
their dead. Their home life was, in fact, the
most precious part of their heritage from their
Virginian and Carolinian and English ancestors.
The rapid acquirement of wealth by growing
cotton did certainly for a time diminish in the
Cotton states the association of wealth with
good birth which had prevailed in the seaboard
states ; but the somewhat patriarchal form which
plantation life always took counteracted any

tendency to develop a recognizable *nouveaux riches* class. The immense size of the planta-tions made it impossible for masters to main-tain with all their slaves that kindly relation of protector and protected, of strong and weak, which was the Virginian tradition. But such a kindly tradition was certainly the rule in planta-tion households, whatever may have been the rule or practice among overseers and field hands.

As we have seen, the great majority of white men owned either no slaves at all, or but one or two. Yet it is true that the plantation was the typical community of the lower South, its laws and usages quite as dominant socially as its economic influence was dominant politically; and the plantation of the lower South, like the plan-tation of Virginia, unfruitful as it was in art and literature and philanthropy, was yet the source of more cordiality and kindliness in all the ordinary relations of men and women, of more generous impulses, of a more constant protest against commercialism, of more distinc-tion of manner and charm of personality, than any other way of life practised by Americans be-fore the Civil War. Men crowded together in new cities, seeking chiefly money, in no wise rooted to the soil, thrown into no permanent relations of superior and inferior, could not be expected to develop those intangible, indefinable social qualities which made Southerners of the planter class intelligible and companionable to English country gentlemen, not because of their birth, but because of their habits of life and thought and speech. One who seeks to understand why, in 1861, the English upper classes favored the South, will not reach the end of his list of causes until he compares such a man as Thomas Dabney, of Mississippi, — his *chevalier* look, his leisurely, easy bearing, his simple and yet graceful courtesy, and his speech, freed of all jarring consonant sounds, — with one of those straightforward, businesslike, equally masterful but less gracious men of the West, who, without practising a bow or sparing a consonant, came forward to tell England and the world that the most picturesque of American institutions was not American at all. It is a superficial historical philosophy which dilates on the economic and institutional differences between the two sections, and ignores such smaller divergences as appeared in the manners and speech of individuals.

The harshness of the outward, the militant aspect of the civilization of the lower South, the gentleness and charm of the inner side of plantation life, make a contrast hard for a stranger to understand. But to one who, in the gloomy years of the slow upbuilding of that overthrown and prostrate civilization, has sought to see it as it was before it fell, — to one who has studied men's faces which, however they hardened after laughter, were yet always quick to lighten up with kindliness and merriment, and women's faces which, however marked with the touch of sorrow and humiliation and an unfamiliar poverty, were yet sealed with a true seal of dignity and grace, — to such a student of the old Southern life, the inner side of it is more attractive than the outer. The one is like the midday look of that fruitful but too heated land; the other brings to mind its evening aspect. Those midday heats are often hard to bear. The sun's progress through the heavens is the hard march of a ruthless conqueror. The rank vegetation fairly chokes the earth. Insects buzz and sting and irritate. Serpents writhe to the surface of miasmous streams. Beasts palpitate and grow restless. Men brood,

and weary of the loneliness, and long for excitement, for fierce deeds, battles, conquests. But with
the sudden dropping of the sun in the West a swift
change comes over the earth and beasts and
men. There is the stillness of the wide, level
fields, snowlike with cotton; the softer, night-
time noises of the woods and swamps; the splen-
dor of the Southern stars; the tinkling of banjos
and the twinkling of lights in the negro quarters; the white dresses of women and children,
and the exquisite, slow tones of human voices
on the verandas of the great house. The rancor of the midday passes — eclipsed, overcome, atoned for, by the charmed sweetness of
that dying hour.

# THE ASCENDENCY OF THE LOWER SOUTH IN THE UNION

In order to understand the nature and the magnitude of the effect which the rise of the Cotton states had upon the political history of the whole country, it is necessary to recall the general political situation when senators and representatives from the lower South first took their seats in Congress ; to realize how definite and single their controlling motive in public life was; to analyze the sources of the power they wielded; and to do justice to the ability and zeal, however misguided it may have been, of the men themselves.

Taking the close of Monroe's second administration in 1824 as our point of departure, we find it a time when any strong and definite material interest, adequately represented at Washington, was sure to have a powerful influence on the course of affairs. With the passage of the great men of the revolutionary school there passed also, for a time at least, the great questions they had dealt with. The second war with Great Britain had divorced us, far more conclusively than the first, from those European complications against which Washington and Jefferson had warned their countrymen. Our Constitution had been operating long enough and well enough to inspire a general confidence in its soundness and to discourage any attempt to alter its essential features. The relations between the different departments of the government had been fixed with reasonable finality. Hamilton had done his work so well that the finances no longer required any heroic treatment or provoked any bitter controversies. The Federalist party, having served the purpose of its founding, and exhausted its energy in the work of construction, and having shown its inability to adapt itself to the new conditions which its own policies had brought about, had practically disappeared. There was little discussion of principles, and as yet no clear alignment on policies and interests. It is misleading to say, as so many historians do say, that only one party existed, but party lines had been obscured. Ceasing to divide on the old questions, men did not know how they were going to divide on questions which did not yet present themselves clearly. So they broke into factions, grouping about leaders instead of fighting for causes.

The new questions were not yet clearly formulated because, as the country turned from a foreign war to consider its own internal life and growth, no great conflict of material interests was yet clearly manifest. New England, though first the embargo and then the war had sadly diminished that seafaring industry of hers which Burke praised so, was not yet sure that her industrial future was to be mainly an affair of mills and shops. Kentucky and the middle West, and even Virginia and the seaboard Southern states, still entertained hopes of a various industrial development, based on their variety of material resources. It was in Kentucky and the middle West that the policy of protection and internal improvements, the "American system," had had its birth, and Henry Clay was its champion. By the side of Clay there had stood the young Calhoun, of South Carolina, those fierce eyes of his aglow with a true national spirit, while the young Webster had opposed them both, exposing the fallacies and combating the whole theory of protection with the most massive elo-

quence ever arrayed against it. If there was
one quarter of the Union where the new national feeling was weak, it was New England,
her old Federalist leaders long excluded from
power, her industry not yet diverted from its
ancient channels, her best minds not yet quick-
ened by the Unitarian revolt into those successive experiments of a larger and larger intellectual
freedom which began with the leadership of
Channing and culminated in the leadership of
Garrison. Virginia was already in that hesitat-
ing, divided state, torn by the conflict between
her traditions of spacious patriotism and her
institutional kinship with the lower South, which,
even more than the decline of her public men,
debarred her from leadership for forty years.
If there was one quarter of the Union where
the new national feeling was strongest, it was
the middle West, where Clay led, and the Southwest, where Andrew Jackson, shrewdly coached,
was turning his military glory into political
power. South Carolina was beginning to bring
to bear upon Calhoun that detaining urgency
from the rear which first checked him in his
promising career as a national statesman, and
set him thinking about the nature of the gov-

ernment, and finally turned him into the very
type and exemplar of fidelity to a special interest.

How strong that interest was first appeared in
the debates over the admission of Missouri.
Northern men were not at that time moved by any
such aggressive antislavery impulse as appeared a
decade or more later. They were acting just as
Jefferson acted in regard to the Northwest territory, and in accordance with his views. What
startled the country now, and startled the aged
Jefferson himself, was the fierceness of the opposition to his own programme of limiting slavery to
the states where it already existed : the Southern
congressmen and senators were almost solidly in
favor of admitting Missouri as a slave state. However, with the adoption of Clay's compromise, the
rancor quickly subsided. There was for a time
general acquiescence in the decision that a geographical line should divide the regions in which
slavery existed and into which it might spread
from the regions into which only free labor should
be admitted. We may, therefore, take the compromise as a sort of law of war, fixing the terms on
which all sectional contests which might arise in
the ordinary course of legislation should be fought

out. For a clear illustration of the long conflict of interests which now began, and a setting forth of the interest which the men of the Cotton states particularly represented, it is better for us to turn to the tariff controversy from 1828 to 1833. It was over such questions as the tariff and finance and foreign affairs, — ordinary subjects of legislation,— and not over the admission of new states, that the fight was made during the years immediately following the rise of the lower South.

Clay was still the champion of the American system, but Calhoun was now against him, and Webster's great figure was by his side. Webster was unquestionably influenced by the material interests of his section, now pursuing chiefly manufactures and domestic commerce; and Calhoun by the material interests of his, now committed to agriculture and to an exchange of one or two staples, preferably with Europe, for all other products of industry. That these two eminent men and their associates and followers were so influenced cannot be accounted a positive reproach, for the great majority of public men have always stood mainly for material interests. In our national Congress to-day the representatives of each sec-

tion and each corner of the country feel that it is
their first concern to protect and advance its material interests.   For this they are ordinarily sent to
Washington and kept there.   Let any one of them
neglect this, and he will ordinarily lose his seat.
Some are no doubt wise enough to see that the
highest interests of every section are bound up in
the welfare of the whole, and all but a very few
have theories and sympathies of their own which
they express in their votes and speeches, so far as
they can express them without antagonizing the
interests they represent.   Occasionally, too, a
statesman altogether devoted to the national honor
and integrity, or to a single principle, keeps his
place by virtue of exceptional ability and popu-
larity.   But such men are not common.   Of that
limited class of public men, Clay and Jackson were
representatives at the time of which I am speaking,
and Webster and Calhoun, though both probably
superior intellectually to Clay and Jackson, were
not.   Neither were the new men from the new
Southern states who now appeared in Washington.
Many of them were at first supporters of Jackson,
and some stood for a while with Clay.   But it was
not many years before they came to act as a rule
with Calhoun and McDuffie, of South Carolina,

whenever there was a clear conflict between the interest they represented and any other interest whatsoever.

What these men of slow voices and leisurely bearing and great capacity for intimate personal relationships and inbred fondness for power stood for at Washington was not slavery alone, not cotton and rice and sugar-cane alone, not agriculture alone, but the whole social organism, the whole civilization, whose decay in Virginia had been arrested by the rise of the states from which they came. They were committed to the maintenance, in the most progressive country in the world, of a primitive industry, a primitive labor system, and a patriarchal mode of life. They held that their main industry could be successfully prosecuted only with slave labor, and while it was so prosecuted it tended to exclude all other forms of industry. Its economic demands were imperative; its political demands were hardly less imperative. Economically, it demanded that the fewest possible restrictions be placed upon the exchange of its two or three staple products for the products of other countries, and that it be permitted to extend itself constantly to fresh lands. Politically, it demanded protection from criticism and from social and humanitarian reforms and changes. In order to enforce these economic and political demands, the representatives of the plantation interest must do more than stand on the defensive. They must not merely resist attack, they must prevent it. They must not only hold their own with the representatives of other sections, they must take the lead in the nation. They must be not the equals merely, but the superiors, of Northern public men. In a word, they must rule.

The compelling demand behind them, the definite and specific nature of their task, was itself, in a time of obscured party divisions and but half understood antagonisms, a principal cause of their success. They had, further, the advantage of representing in Congress property as well as men; for three-fifths of the slaves were counted in apportioning representatives to different states, and the slaves were, to all intents and purposes, save in politics, property, and not men. Particular Southern states counted the three-fifths of the slaves in laying out congressional districts and added only enough whites to make up a proper constituency. Whoever represented such a district at Washington was sure to be heartily committed to the Southern system.

Moreover, the Cotton states were sure of the support of Virginia and the upper South. However ·the plantation system might decay there, whether the agricultural interest controlled there or not, the slaveholding interest was sure to be on their side; for the slaveholder of the upper South knew that the value of his slaves depended, not on the profits of his own tobacco plantation, but on the demand for slave labor on the rice and sugar and cotton plantations farther south. Very frequently, he sent numbers of his slaves southward, not to be sold, but to cultivate under an overseer a plantation of his own. The kinship of ideas and social usages between the two halves of the South was scarcely less potent than this partial identity of interests; and if more were needed, there was the strong tie of blood kinship as well. The older line of a Virginian family, clinging to its first seat in the tide-water region, was not likely to antagonize the younger line in its new seat, modelled after the old, on the Mississippi or the Alabama.

Allies in the North were not hard to find. There were manufacturers taking the places of the old merchant princes in the East, the fabric of whose fortunes was largely based on cotton; and there were other manufacturers, and merchants as well, who found in the South as it was a sure and paying market, which might be lost somehow if the agitators had their way. It is not difficult to understand why abolitionism was so long associated with incendiarism and vagabondage in the East, or why there were so many clean shirts and broadcloth coats in the mobs that threatened Garrison and Phillips. In the West and Northwest, a similar material interest could be relied on. The Northwestern farmer was bound to the lower South not merely by the fact that cotton was easily convertible into cash to pay for his breadstuffs and his beef and bacon; his interest also lay in the Southerner's refusal to make more than one appeal to the soil. He may never have reasoned the matter out, but he knew where his products went and he did not wish his customers disturbed. Moreover, the southern counties of the states above the Ohio were colonized largely by men of the Virginian stock, and Cincinnati and other rising Western cities owed to trade with the South almost as much of their prosperity as the country regions owed of theirs. Finally, there were to be found everywhere throughout the North devoted adherents of the principle of state

rights who could be counted on for help whenever
the Southerners cried out against interference in
their affairs; and there were many, though not
so many, conservatives, who had their misgivings
about the rapid extension of the suffrage — steadfast supporters of the rights of property, who were
sure to frown upon any revolutionary movements
directed against vested interests. With the first
class, Southern Democrats could always form
alliances; with the second class, Southern Whigs
were equally sure of fellowship.

But when all these helps to leadership have been
considered, one must still study the men of the
lower South themselves in order to understand why
they were so long successful against the economic
and moral forces they had to fight with — against
the whole tendency of modern thought, against the
whole trend of American progress, against the true
spirit of liberty. Early in the century, a speaker
of the House of Representatives declared that he
found himself embarrassed about committee assign-
ments because there were so many representatives
from the state of South Carolina whose abilities
and experience gave them claims to the leading
places. Calhoun's preëminence in South Carolina
was not universally admitted until Lowndes was

dead; and it is doubtful if, a little later, even Calhoun's subtle reasoning on constitutional questions should be rated higher than George McDuffie's thorough mastery of the economics of the tariff discussion. The public men of the Gulf states were in some cases men who had first appeared in politics in the seaboard states; they were nearly always trained politicians of a school far different from that in which the merely clever and industrious machine politicians of our time are trained. They usually came into politics from the law, or from the headship of a plantation. If from the law, they might be self-made men, with the self-made man's hardihood and independence, yet they were apt to have acquired, as Andrew Jackson, and Calhoun, and McDuffie, for example, did acquire, the distinction of manner common to the large-planter class. If from the plantation, they were usually men who had successfully withstood the temptations of power and wealth and solitude; and such men were the only class in America corresponding in character to the hereditary ruling class in other countries. The power and place which the owner of land and slaves in the Cotton states had might make a weak man weaker, but they were as sure to make a strong man stronger.

If the same conditions which in colonial Virginia
starved out common schools and limited the intellectual development of the mass of landless white
men did yet breed Washington and Henry, those
conditions, intensified in the lower South, were as
sure to breed strong leaders there as they were to
limit the development of the mass. A study of the
portraits and photographs of Southern statesmen
of the old régime inspires one with the respect we
always give to strength. These, one says of
them, are such faces as might have belonged to
the markgräfen of mediæval Germany, to the lords
of the marches in England and Scotland, or to
those generals who, in the later ages of the Roman
Empire, so often beat back the forces that have
made modern Europe what it is.

It is illuminating to review in outline the course
these men took, and the power they exercised,
on the great permanent questions which were so
often debated during our period — the questions of
taxation and revenue, internal improvements, public
finance, and foreign affairs.

It was on the tariff question that they first
showed how much firmer they were than the
Virginians and Kentuckians. South Carolina, an
old state, and like Virginia, somewhat weakened, in

the matter of the energy of her men, by the south-westward emigration, felt more keenly than the new states the pinch that always came to a land exploited by the plantation system. Her most virile young men were apt to emigate; her best lands were exhausted. Moreover, Charleston, which had once bid fair to rival New York, still had possibilities of importance under free trade. McDuffie, of South Carolina, set forth first and most clearly the reason why protective tariffs could not fail to bear unequally on the Cotton states. A tax on their imports, he declared, was in effect a tax on their exports. They themselves had nothing to protect. Their main product met with no dangerous competition either at home or abroad. The tariff duties imposed on their tools, their furniture, and everything else they got from England, might as well be imposed directly on the cotton they exported to pay for those things. Imposed either way, it meant simply that a bale of cotton would purchase fewer of the things which they wanted, and which they preferred to buy in England rather than in New York or Boston. To reply that the Cotton states could profit from protection by varying their industries was in effect to say that they could do so by changing their whole labor system and the whole constitution of their society.

The reasoning was perfectly sound, and practically the whole lower South approved it. But the plan to enforce the reasoning by nullifying a law and threatening secession did not get the approval of the whole lower South. The mass of the public men even of the Cotton states were still too much dominated by a genuine patriotism, and too devoted adherents of Andrew Jackson, to go so far as their South Carolinian leaders, Calhoun and McDuffie, were ready to go. The fight that South Carolina made for an economic principle was not entirely unsuccessful. The fight she made for a constitutional theory was lost. Her defeat was due to the greater prosperity, the greater hopefulness, and the genuine patriotism which prevailed in the younger states; her victory was due to the solidarity of all the Cotton states behind her on the economic question. Their congressmen voted for the compromise tariff of 1833, and constantly favored the antiprotective plan of ad valorem duties. When, after a long period of financial depression and failing revenues, higher duties were imposed, they

saw to it that the principle of protection got no
more countenance than it did in 1842. It was
Walker, of Mississippi, who in 1846 prepared the
treasury report on tariff taxation which is oftenest
contrasted with Hamilton's; and the tariff law
framed and passed by the Congress to which
that report was addressed, whatever the actual
rate of duties might seem to indicate, was
more clearly in accordance with the principles
of free trade, more clearly contrary to protec-
tionist ideas and devices, than any other tariff
law since 1789. The victory could never have
been won, in the face of the development of
those interests in the North which in later years
have defeated or baffled every movement toward
free trade, but for the more compact and solid
front which the representatives of the plantation
interests of the South — the only important body
of interests aggressively opposed to protection
— presented, through a long term of years, alike
to Clay's followers in the West and to Webster's
followers of the East. The victory bade fair to
be a permanent one. Even Sumner, of Massachusetts, voted in 1857 for a tariff as distinctly
revenue in principle as that of 1846 and far
lower in its general rate of duties. Protection

was not revived until the lower South ceased to be represented at Washington.

The other half of Clay's American policy fared no better. On the question of internal improvements, as on the tariff question, Calhoun was with him until it clearly appeared that the Cotton states were to have no part in that general industrial development which the second war with Great Britain, by forcing us to depend on ourselves, had done so much to start, and which Clay's policies were meant to promote. But an influence far more powerful than Calhoun's was enlisted against the policy of internal improvements, as it would doubtless also have been enlisted against protection but for the method which the Carolinians took to fight it. Jackson himself early came to the conclusion that Congress had no right to appropriate money for the Maysville road. Like Monroe, he based his veto on constitutional grounds; and no doubt the constitutional objection had great weight with the majority of Southern men in Congress, who first sustained such vetoes, and then, growing stronger and stronger, often relieved the successors of Jackson of the responsibility of the veto by defeating similar measures in one house

or the other. But the economic consideration,
I feel sure, was also potent, though vaguely. Internal improvements and high tariffs went hand
in hand; they were policies sprung from the
same general motive and principle, and the
same impulse that set the representatives of
the plantation system against the one set them
against the other also. The cotton planter felt
that he paid more than his share of the expense
of governmental enterprises, and he also felt
that he got less than his share of the benefits.
It is not probable that he made even to himself a confession of the weakness of his industrial system which would prevent his getting
a fair share of the fruits of a national policy,
but he may have felt, as unstudious citizens
often do, an antagonism of interests which he
did not clearly reason out. A direct consequence
of opening highways and dredging rivers and
improving harbors is to thicken population, and
the plantation system made for sparseness of
population. Another effect is to build up cities,
and few cities so built up were likely to arise
below Mason and Dixon's line. In a word, the
great majority of internal improvements could
fully justify themselves, and confer the maximum

of benefits, only where industry could be diversified. They would benefit the new states of the Northwest, given over to free labor, far more than they could benefit the lower South.

The attempts to revive the policy after its first overthrow grew feebler and feebler. A recent historian of political parties thinks that the Whigs might have had a better chance after 1850 if they had taken it up vigorously again. But almost the last words Clay ever pronounced in the senate-chamber were spoken in vain defence of a river and harbor bill carrying less than two and a half million dollars. The policy could not be revived successfully until the Cotton states withdrew from the Union. Only their withdrawal, and the subsequent military conquest of them, and the overthrow of their industrial system, made it possible for a different set of industrial interests so to control Congress and the courts that nowadays a river and harbor bill, carrying tens of millions, encounters its most serious obstacle in the desire of individual congressmen to increase the total with provisions for the benefit of their particular districts and states.

On questions of public finance, the influence of the men of the Cotton states, though not, perhaps, so controlling an influence, was a very strong one; and in two very clear ways the plantation system helped to determine the course of Southern public opinion and public men on such questions.

The first way was by preventing the growth of great cities. At the present time, no student of public finance needs to be told that the cities and the country districts are apt to take contrary sides in financial discussions, though the alignment has varied markedly from time to time in our history. The Southern people had, as a rule, a country view and not a city view of finance. The second way in which the plantation system had its effect in such controversies was more definite. It made it necessary to transact most of the business of exchange, and so created a strong demand for money, at one time of year, — the harvest time, — while in other seasons there was very little business requiring the use of a medium of exchange. If the cotton planter found money scarce at the harvest time, he got less for his product, and had lesser balances accredited to him on the books of his agent at New Orleans or Mobile or Charleston; but if the money supply increased at other seasons, he was a loser, because of the heightened charges entered against him in his agent's books for the tools and supplies advanced to him while he planted and tended the next crop. This consideration was strong in all agricultural communities, but strongest where but one great crop was grown, and where agriculture was the only important industry. What the planters of the country chiefly desired, therefore, and the cotton planters most of all, was a currency that could be expanded during the brief business season in the autumn. They naturally favored state banks, because they were more amenable to the demands of regions remote from the great centres of business than a national bank or any system of national banks could well be. Their remoteness from the great centres, and their unfamiliarity with large business operations, naturally inspired them with fear and distrust of such an institution as the Bank of the United States. A few of the larger planters, who had a liking for such institutions as seemed clearly to promote the stability of the country, and an affiliation with propertied men of all sections, probably did not share this fear. But as Mr. Cairnes points out, the very largest planters were generally borrowers, because their constant tendency was to enlarge their holdings, and so they, as well as other classes in the Cotton states, were generally drawn to favor state banks, with abundant power to issue notes and lend them on all sorts of securities. President Jackson got much support from the South throughout his long fight with the national bank. All the states of the lower South had their bank systems, their flush times, and their experiments of cheap money, and all suffered severely from the collapse and reaction that followed. That experience the West had also, and the blame for the state banks cannot be put upon the South alone. But the growth of population and of cities in the West brought about a different feeling there on questions of finance, while the South remained as it was. As to the national bank, the successive attempts to revive it were usually opposed by Southern opinion and resisted by the mass of Southern public men. As we know, those attempts were not successful, and in finance, as in the matter of tariffs and internal improvements, the so-called national policy was not revived until the lower South was no longer represented in Congress.

On these great domestic questions, then, the power of the lower South was exercised quite consistently on the side which Jefferson would most probably have taken. It was directed, in general, against those forces which tended to strengthen the government at Washington. And yet, when the old Republican party was divided, the great planters and their associates did not, as a rule, join the Democratic party. On the contrary, probably a majority of them were Whigs. We know, at least, that in most Southern states the districts which usually returned Whigs to Congress were the districts in which the big plantations, the rich black lands, and the bulk of the slaves were found. These men were influenced by such general considerations and sympathies, and maintained such a generally conservative attitude toward society, as would have made them Tories in England. Still, whether the great planter was a Whig or a Democrat, he usually stood with his fellows whenever the interests of his section or his class were clearly threatened, and so did the Southern Whigs at Washington.

But the greatest of the victories which the plantation interest won at Washington was not won in the advocacy of a Jeffersonian weak-government policy, but of a policy which, as we have been often told of late, inevitably tends to

strengthen a national government at the expense
of smaller communities, no less than at the expense
of the liberty of individuals.   These triumphs were
won in the foreign relations of the Republic.   The
power of the plantation and the slave availed not
merely to keep the government from doing things
but also to make the government do things of a
very positive sort.   It could lower tariffs, and stop
the progress of the Maysville road, and overthrow the bank ; it could also organize armies and
fleets, it could extend our limits, it could play a
part in that world movement of the English stock
which we to-day understand so much more clearly,
and approve or condemn so much more intelligently, than we ever did before.

It would be a mistake to attribute the course of
the public men of the lower South on domestic
questions entirely to the economic demands of their
industrial system, ignoring the character, the political connections, the inherited sympathies and
tendencies, of the people.   Similarly, it would be
a mistake to attribute their course on foreign
questions entirely to the demand for fresh lands
for slavery to spread into, clearly as we can suit
the effect to the cause.   In this also, less plain,
less definite forces were at work.   Expansion is

characteristic of young and strong peoples; it
is a marked characteristic of the English-speaking
peoples. Of the two or three white stocks that
peopled the lower South, not one was wanting in
the adventurous pioneer impulse; indeed, the
generalization is reasonably true of the whole
American people up to the time of which we are
speaking. In the North, that impulse spent itself
somewhat in business. In the South, what took the
place of business was not of a nature to satisfy
it. Moreover, the South was closer to those
Latin-American States which alone, in those days
before the Golden Gate of the Pacific had been
opened, tempted adventurous Americans with
their weakness and their show of wealth. What
wonder, then, that the Southern planter, moody
with the loneliness and monotony of his life, felt
within him, from time to time, stirrings of the old
adventurous spirit? What wonder if, even though
his peculiar social system gave within a few years
a look of antiquity to communities whose whole
life was compassed by the lifetime of one man, he
soon longed for fresh experiences, enemies to fight,
strange civilizations to penetrate and overthrow?
Into the dull recitative of his plantation days there
broke, again and again, the bold, clear notes of

the old buccaneer theme.  He could not, like Ralegh and Drake and Hawkins, pursue his race ideal over the salt seas, but the mystery of the Southwestern plains was not less tempting.  That way, too, the track of the Spaniard led; and to the southeastward, almost in sight from the Florida coast, were other Spaniards to despoil.  Arkansas, the last of the Southern states to be carved out of the Louisiana purchase, was not yet in the Union, when men like Bowie and Travis and Crockett and Houston were already in Texas. A little later, filibuster expeditions were landing on the coast of Cuba, and the public men of the lower South at Washington, turning more and more from small things to great, were directing American diplomacy to the purchase of Cuba and the annexation of Texas.

No doubt, the economic and political exigencies of slavery had their part in all this.  Already, in the forties, some lands were exhausted even in so new a country as Alabama.  To maintain its equality in the Senate, the South must get more slave states somewhere.  But surely it is not necessary to attribute to a particular and reasoned motive alone what resulted before, and has resulted since, from a simple and general impulse.  In the

face of very recent history, it is hard to deny that
the filibusters and the Texans were doing just
what their ancestors had been doing for four
hundred years, and what we did but yesterday. If
we look for a parallel to the Alamo, where none
would fly while escape was possible, and not one
man yielded when all hope of victory was gone, or
to Crittenden's desperate enterprise in Cuba, we
find it in no land battle, but in the last fight of
the *Revenge*, and Grenville's order to the master-
gunner "to split and sinke the shippe; that thereby
nothing might remaine of glorie or victorie to the
Spaniards." Slavery had to do with the seizure
of Texas and the attempts upon Cuba. But we
may not attribute to that alone this single act in
the long drama which began before the first slave
landed in Virginia and ended in 1898. The true
cause of it was that old land hunger which half
the world has not satisfied. If Southern adventurers and Southern statesmen took the lead in it,
their leadership was due to their whole training
and character and life; it was not due entirely to
the fact that they were slave-owners, and that
slavery must keep spreading or perish.

In Texas, they had their way with little difficulty. The first fight, for the independence of the

state, being won, the second fight, for annexation, was sure to go in their favor. We all know how Tyler was brought into line for annexation; how Clay, in his last effort to win the presidency, lost the votes of the Free-soil men by disclaiming, in certain letters to an Alabama slaveholder, all opposition to admitting Texas save from the fear that the Union might be endangered; and how, as against Polk, an avowed annexationist, he failed to win any votes by his concession to the lower South. When the last act came on, and Mexico had to be conquered, it was mainly volunteers from the Cotton states, joined by a few of their Northern friends, like Franklin Pierce, who swelled our little army to the strength the enterprise demanded. As it happened, Taylor, who fought his way to the presidency in that war, was a Louisianian and a planter, and among those who followed him was his son-in-law, Jefferson Davis. Quitman, who had once resigned his place as governor of Mississippi in order to stand a trial for filibustering, raised the flag over the city of Mexico. A host of new names, with which the whole world rang a few years later, were first made known by honorable mention in the despatches. The whole enterprise, from the

Alamo to Cherubusco, and all that came of it
in new territories and new states, was part of
the record of the lower South's ascendency in
the Union.

But the sailing in Cuban waters was rougher
then than it has proved in our time. Northern
opposition did not indeed prevail in that matter any
more than in the Texas movement. It was conciliated or beaten down so effectually that Buchanan could be elected President after signing the
Ostend Manifesto, which declared that, if Spain
refused to sell us Cuba, necessity, and particularly
military necessity, might justify us in seizing it.
But filibustering failed. Soulé, the fiery Creole,
sent to Madrid with a special view to getting us
Cuba, found duelling pistols and small swords no
more effective instruments than notes and mani-
festos against Spain's firm resolve to keep her
hold on the island which seemed so ready to fall
into our grasp. For once, the ancient enemy prevailed; and none of us can fail to admire the pride,
the dignity, the majesty, of the defiance she sent
back to us then, even in the light which has since
been thrown upon her weakness. It is curious that
the first reverse the men of the lower South ever
met in their thirty years of rule and conquest should

have come from such a source. The contrast is
striking between their steady and masterful progress to their end in the controversy with Mexico
and the fiasco which came of every attempt they
made upon Cuba.

But in all things else their ascendency at Washington at the middle of the century was clearer
than ever. Save when a president died in office,
the White House was generally occupied either
by a Southerner of their own band or by a Northern man of their choice. In the lower House of
Congress, the great committees were commonly
headed by their representatives. Two chairmen
of the Ways and Means Committee came from the
particular Cotton state of which I have spoken.
In the Senate, as Calhoun and Webster and Clay
successively disappeared, the true leaders were
such men as Butler, of South Carolina, Toombs
and Cobb, of Georgia, Benjamin and Soulé, of
Louisiana, William R. King, and C. C. Clay, of
Alabama, and Jefferson Davis of Mississippi. The
representatives and senators from New England, many of them able and accomplished men,
had no more leadership than their predecessors
had in those days, just before the reply to Hayne,
when a New England congressman could be rec-

ognized by his deprecatory manner. Western men were frequently in alliance with the Southerners, as in the case of Douglas and Cass. Men from the Middle states, like Buchanan, went even farther to promote their ends. Those who occasionally stood out against them did so at the expense of any ambition they might entertain for the highest places. In cabinet after cabinet, the leading places went to them and their friends. The Supreme Court, under Taney, was as little likely to thwart them as Congress or the President, for the majority of the court was now guided by Jefferson's ideas of the government, instead of Marshall's.

It remains for us to follow them in the fight they had to make for the fruits of their victories — to see them meeting a resistance, for the first time truly firm and wise, which in the Northwest enlarged into a great political movement that which in the Northeast had been merely a protest. We shall see them trampling upon the antislavery sentiment of New England, only to find the hateful seed bursting out of Western prairies vaster than their own Black Belt. We shall see them profiting in election after election by the folly of Free-soilers and Liberty men, only to suffer by the rise of the Republicans. We shall see them hanging John Brown with all the right forms and generous delays of a just law, only to face, over the grave of a misguided visionary, that practical, reasonable, pliant, and unconquerable force of public opinion which Abraham Lincoln, sprung obscurely from their own Virginian line, was sent into the world to summon up, to guide, to restrain, and to obey.

## THE FINAL STRUGGLE IN THE UNION

OUR examination, though it be not in detail, of the civilization of the Cotton states, and of the effects of the rise of those states on the political history of the whole country up to the year 1850, permits us now to examine, still in broad outline, the motives, the character, and the larger significance of the last struggle which the champions of that civilization made to maintain its political ascendency in the Union. The struggle for ascendency was, in fact, a struggle for existence. As I have tried to point out, the lower South was from the beginning under a necessity either to control the national government or radically to change its own industrial and social system.

Let us first, still keeping, so far as possible, our inside point of view, and looking out upon the whole country from the windows, as it were, of the civilization which we have been studying, try to see what dangers the Southerner of 1850 had to guard against, what enemies he had to fight.

On nearly all of the domestic questions debated

between 1820 and 1850, the men of the lower
South had been on that side which a certain general theory of government, the Jeffersonian Democratic theory, might have led them to take, and did
lead many Northern men to take, quite without reference to sectional interests and antagonisms. That
general theory undoubtedly had great weight with
the Southerners themselves. We know that Southerners could be so influenced, for a contrary general view of the government prevailed quite ap-
preciably among Southerners of certain classes,
although in cases of a clear conflict of sectional
interests over specific subjects the conflict of general theories among themselves rarely availed seriously to divide the men of the lower South, however it might divide the men of Virginia and the
border states. Nevertheless, as we have seen, the
course of the lower South on these great domestic
questions was also in accord with the economic and
political demands of its civilization, and it must be
said that its public men had their way on all of
them.

In consequence, there was now no serious
threat to their civilization from the tariff, from the
policy of internal development and improvement, or
from the system of public finance. Whether or

not those general principles on which the public
men of the Cotton states had acted in domestic
affairs while they were ruling the country were
just principles, good for the whole country, at
least the North made, in 1850, no such resistance to their policies as to reveal any clear conflict of industrial interests or to show any reason
why, so far as the tariff, finance, and ordinary
governmental enterprises were concerned, the two
social orders, unlike as they were, might not go
on existing side by side under the government at
Washington, so long as the government's energies were confined within the limits assigned to it
by the majority of state rights judges now on the
supreme bench. So long as the North did not
revolt against declining tariff rates, or insistently
demand internal improvements, or try to tear
down the subtreasuries and clamor for a bank, it
could not be said that there was any irrepressible
conflict of an industrial sort. The very unlike-
ness of the two systems seemed to preclude rivalry
while they were confined to separate regions.

So, too, in the matter of foreign relations. No
important Northern interest was distinctly endangered by that aggressive foreign policy which the
Southern leaders initiated in the forties. The

tendency of such a policy to strengthen the national government was certainly not apt to arouse any violent Northern opposition. Its tendency to enlarge the republic physically appealed to a feeling which, however absorption in business and in the occupation of the West may have obscured it, was just as strong in Northern men as in Southern men. It had not as yet led to any great increase in the size and expense of our military and naval establishments. It had brought us into no entanglements or conflicts inimical to the trade of Eastern cities.

So far, then, as hindsight avails us, thoughtful Southerners in 1850 could not have seen, though in point of fact some restless Southern minds persuaded themselves that they did see, any threat to their civilization from specific material interests in the North. Some Southerners did contend that what was left of the protective system was stifling their main industry, which could only grow to its full proportions in an atmosphere of absolute free trade; and some, that manufactures could be developed below Mason and Dixon's line if only that line could be made the boundary between separate nations, and the people south of it·roused to a proper sense of the ignominy of buying ploughs and hoes and furniture and books from Yankees simply because Yankees made them better and sold them cheaper. There were Charlestonians who could not understand why Charleston had stopped growing and New York and Boston had kept on, unless it was because the government somehow helped New York and Boston at the expense of Charleston. Such ideas were often advanced in the Southern commercial conventions, which were held so frequently, and so well attended, that they may be taken to indicate a feeling of industrial unrest and discontent ; but they did not mislead the whole Southern people. Yancey, the Secessionist, once plainly stated a contrary view when he said that in Washington there were two temples, — one for the South, and one for the North. The first was the Capitol, where Southern public men had so long exercised a power out of all proportion to their numbers and to the numbers they represented. The other was the Patent Office, where the untrammelled intellect of the North, dealing with material problems, had registered its triumphs. To make his figure fairer still, he might have joined the National Library to the Patent Office, for the Northern intellect, though it had made no contribution of the first value to the world's inquiry into the things of the spirit, had, nevertheless, already freed America from the reproach of literary barrenness and proved that our civilization could bear other fruit than wealth.

And it was the belated concern of the Northern mind about the things of the spirit, not its absorption in material enterprises, that boded ill to the plantation system. It was the North's moral awakening, and not its industrial alertness, its free thought, and not its free labor, which the Southern planter had to fear. The New England factory made no threat, the town meeting did. The Northwestern wheat farms and pork packeries and railways were harmless; but Oberlin College and Lovejoy's printing-press and the underground railway were different. It was not the actual material ascendency of the North which endangered the plantation system, though sooner or later, by sheer weight of population, the political ascendency of the South might have been overcome. The true danger from without was in the moral and intellectual forces which were at once the cause and the result of the North's progress. It was in that freedom of individual men which had made the North prosper, and in that national feeling, that national theory of the government, that national antagonism to whatever was weak or alien under the flag, which had resulted from the development and the denser peopling of the North. The final conflict came only when these things were thrown clearly into competition with the picturesque Old World social system, the limited nationalism, the unprogressive industrial contrivances of the South for the occupation of new lands. The frontal attacks of the abolitionist light brigade could enrage and annoy the planter, but they could not seriously weaken the plantation system. The Free-soil emigrant could and did endanger it.

But he did not overthrow it. The end, unlike as it was in the way it came about to the abolitionists' fevered fancies, was equally unlike the emigrant's saner forethought. It did not come through the slow dying out of a thing that must spread or perish. It came through the defiant act of the Southerners themselves. The revolt of the North could have done no more than put slavery on the way to extinction; that was Lincoln's hope, as it had been Jefferson's. We cannot see clearly what actually happened unless we again go inside of Southern civilization, observe the forces that threatened it from within, and humanly un-

derstand what purposes and impulses governed
the Southerners themselves while they were fighting these as well as the enemies from without.

For notwithstanding all the triumphs they had
won in legislation, in diplomacy, and on Mexican
battlefields, the people of the lower South were
themselves growing discontent. That which had
happened in Virginia and along the Atlantic seaboard was coming about on the Gulf, though it
was not yet entirely come about, because the
Gulf states were still very young, and only the
richest of their lands were exhausted. But in
the very shrillness and fierceness of the replies
that the men of the South made to every attack
on their system one detects their own restlessness
under its limitations. Let us remember that they
were still the purest representatives on the continent of its very strongest stocks. Unlike the
Spaniards who first explored their lands, and
who, in Mexico and South America, had inter-
mingled and intermarried with weaker races, these
Englishmen and Scotch-Irishmen and French
Huguenots, though they mingled and intermarried
with each other, and got strength thereby, had
guarded themselves, by perpetuating an institution out of keeping with their times, from the very

possibility of anything like equality, not to say
intermingling, with the lesser tribes. There was
never, for them, any danger of that course. The
same institution which hampered them in their
efforts to keep pace with their fellows in the
North and in old England kept alive in them
every impulse and characteristic with which their
fellows had begun.

They did not, as the Virginians had done,
begin to question the wisdom or rightness of their
life. Before they reached that point, Northern
abolitionists had raised the question first. The
abolitionists, like all forerunners and prophets,
were more intent on discharging their message
than on the actual effect of it. They did not
hint and insinuate and reason gently, as even
a man of the world does when he tries to help
his friend out of an error; they did not, like the
true model of all reformers, combine the wisdom of serpents and the harmlessness of doves.
They merely lifted up their voices and spared
not. That they were dealing with the proudest
and most sensitive people in the world did not
occur to them any more than it seems to occur
to those well-meaning persons who, intent mainly
on freeing their own minds and keeping their

own skirts clean, stand afar off and tell the Southerners of our own day how very badly they are doing under the conditions left to them by defeat in war and the reconstruction of their governments by alien hands. Making men the subject of withering editorials and fiercely denunciatory sermons is not a particularly wise way to help them. Objurgation — the objurgatory method of reform — is effective sometimes with weak men, particularly if it is accompanied with a show of force; it is sometimes, I believe, successfully employed with refractory mules. But objurgation from afar off, without any show or threat of force behind it, could hardly accomplish anything with men like those of the lower South. So far as the early abolitionist movement had any effect at all on these men, it was to confirm them in their adherence to an order of things which they, like the Virginians, would surely have come to question when they were made to feel its economic shortcomings. Abolitionism as a force in Northern society was valuable and admirable, leavening the whole mass; it was the right and natural way for the Northern revolt to begin. Abolitionism as it appeared to Southern society was an interference from without, harsh and cruel and unjust, displaying constantly its ignorance of essential facts, and proceeding on lines contrary to the human nature alike of the master, whom it attacked so bitterly, and of the slave himself, who would never have understood its appeal, and who never would have loved the foremost leaders in it any more than those leaders themselves would have relished the close personal relations with Africans which the Southern master did not find unpleasant.

The leading men of the lower South displayed a constantly heightening pride, and a more and more stubborn unwillingness to concede anything whatever to the outside opponents of their system. On the contrary, they set to work vigorously debating the best means of extending it and all possible means of engrafting upon it those modern appliances by which science has revolutionized the methods of production. They tried to bring it into some sort of harmony, crude and primitive as it was, with modern life. They had some reason, some truth, behind them. No industrial system similar to the North's could possibly be established while the main part of the laboring population of the South was made up of ignorant Africans, no matter whether they were slaves or not. Whether Alexander H. Stephens was right or wrong when he said that the South should act on the principle that white men are naturally superior to black men, thirty-five years of freedom have proved, what Lincoln seems to have understood, that the real cause of all the trouble was not slavery, but the presence of Africans in the South in large numbers. The leaders of Southern thought in the forties and fifties were trying to do just what the leading men of the South are trying to do now, viz. : to discover some way or ways by which a society made up of whites and blacks in almost equal proportions can keep pace with a society made up of whites only. Their plan was to keep the blacks at the bottom, the whites on top. It did not succeed very well, but it succeeded better than the plan adopted in Reconstruction times of putting the blacks on top and the whites at the bottom. Whether the third plan of setting both on the same level and letting them work out their destiny side by side will ever, human nature, black and white, being what it is, have a chance to show its superiority to the other two plans, is a question which even to-day no man can answer.

The Southerners of the fifties had not much success in their efforts to improve and extend their industrial system without essentially changing it. They made an especial effort to improve their methods of transportation. Their enthusiasm over railroads was equal to their earlier enthusiasm over banks. In Alabama, the particular Cotton state which I have chosen for purposes of illustration, there was a sort of frenzy over railroads in the middle of the fifties. A whole system of trunk lines was planned, and notwithstanding the vetoes of a sound Jeffersonian Democrat in the governor's office, the state's money and credit were used to promote the enterprise. At the same time, stirred up by the report of an accomplished state geologist, the people began at last to take into serious consideration the great mineral resources which Sir Charles Lyell had noted a decade or two earlier. A young civil engineer was commissioned to survey a railroad through what the legislature called "the mineral region," meaning the region of which Birmingham is now the centre, but he declared that he had no idea where the mineral region was. The governor who signed his commission could not tell him. Nevertheless, the work was done, and it is interesting to know that in Alabama and other Southern states those developments which have come about in our own day were at least planned nearly fifty years ago. Whether the plans could ever have been carried out with slave labor, or whether white labor could have been induced to undertake them, is one of the questions which the Civil War left unsettled. However one may be inclined to answer it, they never were carried out, the schemes and devices of the Southern leaders to add other industries to agriculture without getting rid of slavery never brought any important results, and the civilization of the Cotton states continued to be threatened from within by the same inevitable decay which had come upon Virginia and the Carolinas. That threat, the consciousness of that danger, the restlessness of strong men under it, conspiring with the abolitionist threat from without, had its first important result in the rise of a party in the lower South parallel and comparable to the abolitionist party of the East.

I have said of the abolition movement that so far as its effects on Northern public opinion are concerned, it was an admirable thing, an indispensable thing. It was comparable to the first beginnings of the Protestant revolt against papal abuses,

to the martyrdoms in which the great Puritan revolt
in England had its rise, to the work of Rousseau
and the encyclopedists in France. The strange,
hard, fervid life of New England, though it brought
forth our most notable literature, our chief educational movements, and a great part of our wealth,
found its rightest outburst and culmination in
that unreasoning, unpractical, magnificent assault
upon the very pillars of the social order, en-
dangering the whole if only it might strike the
wrong so long enthroned in high places. The
sense of human brotherhood which Puritanism
had formerly repressed, or turned into religious
fervor; the zeal of a priesthood stripped of its old
authority and no longer confident of the divine
source of its mission; the sudden impulse of
philanthropy in men and women whose own lives
had in them nothing to explain how a slave could
bear his servitude or a master could be other
than cruel; the broodings of long winter evenings
over the outer world which New England had
not yet brought to her own doors; the village
schoolmarm's hidden passion of protest; the free-
thinker's clear-eyed insight into the hollowness of
every appeal to the past for authority to enthrall
the present; the spirit of Brook Farm and the

genius of the town meeting : — all these New
England ideals and impulses went into that
movement, and the movement itself was the beginning of that wider popular movement which
finally freed the North from the rule of the planter.
It was the essence of New England's aspiration,
the last distinctive expression of New England
character.

Few historians have yet found time to follow the parallel movement to the southward.
The Southern leaders in Washington forced
gag rules through Congress to keep out abolitionist petitions. They suborned the postal service to their ends and got abolitionist literature
debarred from the mails. They invaded the North
and dragged slaves back to their plantations.
They browbeat liberty men in Congress. They
hanged John Brown. Whenever they failed to
crush out abolitionism, it was because there was
in the nature of things no way to reach it, not
because Northern public men kept them from
having their will upon it. But the Southern
leaders who had gained and meant to keep the
ascendency at Washington were not so successful
in dealing with the discontent at home. The
secessionist movement in the Cotton states began

as early as the abolitionist movement in New
England, and it won in the end a far clearer
popular victory. Just as abolitionism, although
aimed at the South, was most dangerous immediately to the compromise men of the North, so the
secession movement, aimed at the North, was
from the first a struggle with the moderate men
and the Union sentiment of the South. The abolitionists were willing to endanger the Union in
order to attack slavery and the plantation system; the secessionists were willing to destroy the
Union in order to defend them. Union men,
North and South, drew together when, in the
struggle over the territory acquired from Mexico,
all the antagonisms were at once revealed : when
the industrial system of the North claimed the new
lands because it had proved itself the better system,
while the plantation system demanded them because
it must spread, and because Southern blood had
won them ; when two contrary theories of the national government were set forth to guide Congress
and the courts in dealing with the crisis ; when the
abolitionists cried out against the Constitution as
a covenant with sin, and the fire-eaters heaped
scornful epithets upon Clay and all other devisers
of makeshifts and patchers-up of compromises.

We all know who the leaders of the compromise movement were; we all know who the leaders of the popular movement against compromise in the North were; few of us can now recall even the names of the men who led the movement against compromise in the South. The peacemakers and the abolitionists have their place in history fixed; the fire-eaters are forgotten.

Yet the pen of Garrison and the voice of Phillips had their counterparts in the Cotton states. William Gilmore Sims, Beverly Tucker, and a host of others, defended slavery in the press. Calhoun, on the brink of the grave, muttered fearful prophecies of coming disaster. When he passed from the scene, Davis and Toombs and Quitman took up the cause. But of all these voices of the South, the clearest and the fiercest came from the heart of the Cotton Empire, from Alabama, from William L. Yancey. Neglected by historians, his was yet a leading rôle in the action behind the scenes: for he spoke, not to legislatures nor to Congress, but to the people themselves. If Wendell Phillips was the orator of abolition, if Clay was the orator of compromise, Yancey was the orator of secession. More clearly, more eloquently, and more effec-

tively than any other, he urged that the Cotton
states could not compromise, for compromise was
surrender.    Slavery must have room or perish.
The South must have what it felt to be its right,
or lose its honor.

Garrison and Phillips never had their way.    The
territorial controversy was compromised in 1850
by a plan of Clay's that proposed to leave the
settlement of the question to the people of the
territories themselves when they should be ready to
come into the Union.    A more effective fugitive-
slave law was passed.    Neither New England nor
any other part of the country acted on the theory
that it was right to disregard the claims of the
Union itself because the Union was a compromise
with slavery.    The idea that the destruction of
slavery was more important than the preservation
of the Union was never accepted by any large number of men.    The actual process by which slavery
was in the end overthrown was in fact quite foreign to the purposes of the avowed abolitionists.
They contributed to the result only by arousing
the conscience of the North, not by devising any
plan of action and getting the North to adopt it.

The extreme men in the South were also
defeated, twice defeated.    They were beaten in

1848, when they tried to commit one of the great
parties — the Democratic — to the position that
Congress must guarantee to every slaveholder
the right to go into the new territories with his
property, without regard to the action of any territorial legislature. They were beaten again when,
after Congress had passed Clay's compromise
measures, they appealed to the people of the
Cotton states to resist. The people of the Cotton
states, like the rest of the country, indorsed the
compromise, and waited to see how it would work.
The majority of them seemed to think that the
plantation and the slave were still safe in the
Union; or else, loving the Union, they were willing to risk something in order that they might
continue to live in it.

And then, for a moment, it began to look as if
they were really going to have all they could ask
inside the Union, as if the plantation and the
slave were going to dominate more clearly than
ever in the councils of the Republic. I mean, of
course, when Douglas, a candidate for the presidency, a Northern man with Southern views,
persuaded Congress in 1854 to throw open to
slavery, in the same way that the Mexican cession
was open to slavery, a region which had been

given over to free labor since the compromise of
1820. I have spoken of the Mexican cession as
the crowning triumph of the public men of the
Cotton states, and so it was. The opening of
Kansas to slavery in 1854 was, indeed, a greater
defeat for the antislavery men, a more humiliating
indignity to the opponents of slavery, than anything they had yet endured. But it can hardly
be set down as the achievement of Southern men.
Many moderate slave-owners were in fact surprised
at it. More clearly than almost any other important event in our history, it was the work of one
man — Douglas. Although it came to them as a
consequence of their ascendency, the slave-owners
accepted it as a gift, and not as a reward of their
own labors. Yancey, however, found very few to
agree with him when he contended that even the
gift was unacceptable because it seemed to come
with a reservation in favor of the ultimate right
of the people who might occupy the new territories to say for themselves whether they would
have slavery or not.

But the act of Douglas was in reality fraught
with more immediate danger to slavery than the
events of 1848 and 1850. The Mexican War and
the triumph therein of cotton and slavery had

angered tens of thousands of Northern men ; the
Kansas bill angered hundreds of thousands.   A
year or two later, the Supreme Court of the country ranged itself squarely on the side of the
South ; but a mightier force than Congress, or
courts, or armies, was against it — the force of
public opinion.   Garrison and Phillips had done
their work ;  Clay had done his ;  Douglas, his.
Now at last the slumbering giant was aroused.

Blindly feeling about for a minister who should
give them both their desires, the preservation of
the Union and the destruction of slavery, the
people of the North found Abraham Lincoln, and
the end of dispute and compromise was near.
No longer confined to such methods of opposition as underground railways and personal liberty
bills, which brought them in conflict with the law,
and clearly violated that understanding between
the two sections, — morally binding on many men,
whether or not it was regarded as a compact, —
which was set forth in the Constitution itself,
the antislavery sentiment of the North had at
last a definite and constitutional plan of action.
Free labor poured into Kansas, and the weaker
system went to the wall before the stronger.
The Republican party was formed, not to attack

slavery in the states where it already existed, but
to strangle it by keeping it out of the territories.

But if Northern men thought that the men of
the lower South were going to give up the initiative, and stand merely on the defensive, after
thirty years of power and conquest, they had
profited little by their abundant opportunity to
study the temper of their rulers. In the accounts
of this period by Southern writers, the South is
generally represented as standing entirely on the
defensive, and there is a sense in which that is
true. As I have tried to make plain, they could
not defend their system without controlling the
government. Their attitude was like Sir Anthony
Absolute's in "The Rivals": "You know I am
compliance itself — when I am not thwarted; no
one more easily led — when I have my own way."
They were on the defensive as Lee was on the
defensive when he protected Richmond by invad-
ing Pennsylvania. For my own part, I think
better of those men because, masters so long,
they were masterful to the last. One can rejoice
when a strong man, taking a high and proud
course, is reclaimed and humbled by the sympathy
and tenderness of his friends. But the same man,
if he be merely upbraided and threatened with

punishment, and not even beaten to his knees, and if he yet fall a-whimpering, and promise to mend his ways because he must, fails to command even our aspect. On the contrary, none of us but in his secret soul will admire him more if he go on with the strong hand, if he run his course out, if he fight his fight to a finish, and then turn his face to the wall and die, and give no sign.

Such was, in fact, the course which the Southern leaders took after the failure of the Kansas-Nebraska scheme and the rise of the Republican party. At the time the Kansas-Nebraska Bill passed, Yancey and the secessionists were reduced to a handful. Several Southern states had been carried by the Union men on platforms declaring not merely that there was no occasion to secede, but that there was no right in a state to secede on any occasion. That was in the platform of the Union men in Alabama in 1851. But when it grew clearer and clearer that slave labor could not compete on equal terms with free labor, and that unless something further were done Kansas and the Middle West, like California, were sure to come into the Union as free states, the Southern extremists grew stronger and stronger. Seizing upon the Southern wing of the Democratic party, they committed it to the extreme platform which the whole party had rejected in 1848. Congress must not only give slave labor a free chance in the territories, it must protect it there against the acts of territorial legislatures and any other expression of the settlers' desire to get rid of it.

The theory of secession became at once the uppermost topic of discussion in every one of the Cotton states. It was discussed in conventions, in joint debates, on the streets of the country towns, at every dinner-table. Up to 1850, probably not one man in a hundred anywhere in the Union outside of South Carolina really knew whether he believed in the right of secession or not, any more than we ourselves, before the battle of Manila, knew whether we believed in imperialism or not. The question had not been practical anywhere but in South Carolina since the Hartford Convention of 1814. But by 1860 a majority of the people of the lower South had made up their minds that they did believe in the right, and a majority, though not a great majority, were ready to exercise it if they could not get what they held to be their rights in the territories and if they could not force Northern communities to live up to the letter of the bond and give back their fugitive slaves.

The men of the lower South formulated their demands at the Democratic National Convention at Charleston, and when the Northern majority declined by a few votes to yield them all they asked, they arose and followed Yancey, their spokesman, out of the hall and out of the party. Meeting again at Baltimore, they defiantly named a Southern man on the extreme Southern platform, and the entire lower South ca t its votes for him. Lincoln, elected but not yet in office, made haste to let them know that he would never interfere with slavery and the plantation system in the states where they already existed. But they had learned too well the real hope in his mind, they believed too thoroughly in his own saying that a house divided against itself could not stand. One by one, the states of the lower South held their solemn conventions. The Union men in every one of them made a brave last stand with their backs to the wall. The congressmen at Washington, the men who for so many years, with a bare equality in one house, a minority in the other, had initiated, passed, or prevented legislation, haughtily retired from their places and hastened to Montgomery. So perfect was the unanimity and solidarity of the people behind

them, after the last fight for the Union had been
lost, that within less than a hundred days from
the election which marked the end of their ascendency at Washington they were seated in the
provisional congress of a new government, dividing
among themselves its cabinet portfolios, choosing
a president from their number, and sending envoys
to Washington, to England, to Europe. Prohibiting the foreign slave trade, they thereby sum-
moned Virginia to choose between the Union her
great sons had builded and the civilization which
had its birth on her shores. That summons failing, they fired on Sumter, and the cannonade at
last awoke the mother of States and forced her
to make her choice at once.

Our history has many dramatic episodes in
which men and women play the parts. Here,
however, was the supremely dramatic moment in
the development of the silent forces on the great
stage where states, not men, are the players.
When Virginia roused herself from her trance of
forty years, she awoke to such a conflict of high
motives and passionate impulses, to be beat upon
by such stormy appeals, to be torn with such
contrary aspirations, as no tragedy queen on any
mimic stage ever was beset with. The imperial

commonwealth had fallen on that sleep weakened
with the pain ˙of bearing states, and wearied out
with the toil of setting in order the spacious
mansion which should shelter them. Now, the
instinct of motherhood called her one way, the
safety of the household another. If she turned
to Massachusetts, once her steadfast ally, no
Adams or Hancock answered her. No Henry,
no Marshall, no grave-eyed Washington was there
to step between her and her fighting soul. She
took hurried counsel, and pleaded for time, and
muttered somewhat of old sacrifices made, old
victories won. Her mountain parts chose liberty
and the new order, her comfortable lowlands clung
to the old. While she still hesitated, and only
half consented, her unruly children were already
compassing her about with armies, ranging their
battle line along her northern border, thrusting
the sword into her reluctant hand, pressing an
unsought crown upon her brow. Even Massachusetts, mother of the hardier brood, may not
judge her harshly if at last her motherhood
yielded to that insistent clamor about her knees.

The cause Virginia thus took up was no longer
her own. The only trophies she could win were
monuments. And yet, we may not altogether con-

demn the cause, or the true leaders in it, or the civilization they fought for. In attempting so broad a view of it and them, I have not been unaware of the dangers inseparable from such a method. Inaccuracy, which minute inquiries have to risk, is less harmful than folly, unfairness, unwisdom, against which one who attempts large views must guard. But the more liberal method, if it endanger us of greater error, may also win us more enlightenment than the other. It is only by drawing a wide circle that we can see what that lost cause really was. It was not the cause merely of a single institution or of a particular theory of government. The power which ruled the Union forty years and then tore it asunder was based on history, it was rooted in human nature, it was buttressed by ancient law and usage. It caught hold of our new continent, and made headway against our new ideas, because it found certain material conditions peculiarly adapted to sustain it. Good men and bad men were its instruments, but it did not radically change the quality either of the men whom it lifted up or of the men whom it bowed down.

No American nowadays needs to be told how dangerous to our American experiment that old

Southern civilization was. Nevertheless, he is but half an American who can find no charm in it. The only apology for it is the men it bred, and how strong they were I have tried to indicate. But the best test of them came at the end, when they fought a losing fight as well as they ever fought a winning one; when they put into the field the very best army their race ever marshalled in any cause, on any continent; when Virginia, from her marvellous county of Westmoreland, brought forth and set at its head yet another captain, greater than any Marlborough or Wellington of them all. If we content ourselves with calling that army a band of rebels, and Lee a traitor, we are in danger of glorifying rebellion; we make "traitor" meaningless. If they broke faith with the new order, it was to keep faith with the old. For it was their whole past, it was the whole past of the race, that surged up the Gettysburg heights, — and the whole future stood embattled to withstand the shock. It is enough if such as come up out of the desert — out of the vineyard turned into a desert, and sown with the dragon's teeth — if even they can rejoice that then, as always, the angels of the future were stronger than the angels of the past.

## II. THE ORATOR OF SECESSION

## II

# THE ORATOR OF SECESSION

## A STUDY OF AN AGITATOR

In the study of American history, we seem to have attained a sufficient remoteness from the great antislavery agitators to justify confidence in the estimates of them and their work which historians like Mr. Rhodes and Mr. Schouler have been making for us. In these fresh and careful accounts of the great sectional controversy, Garrison and Phillips take their place close alongside the men of action who carried on the fight in Congress, in the White House, and on the battlefield. It is, therefore, somewhat surprising that the proslavery agitators are generally neglected by the historians of their times. The congressional side of the proslavery fight has been adequately portrayed, and some attention has been given to the governors and other officials in the South who were active champions of the doomed institution. But of the proslavery agitators, properly so called, we know very little. Even Mr. Rhodes, whose account of Southern society exhibits so conscientious a desire to understand the springs of the secession movement, has told us far less than we should like to know of them, and particularly of the man who was foremost in that work.

The fact is not explained by any lack of striking and picturesque features in the man's career, for it was in many ways extraordinary; nor can it be attributed to the failure of his enterprise, for he and his fellows accomplished their immediate purpose. They may at least share equally with Garrison and Phillips and their associates in the responsibility for precipitating the conflict at one time instead of another, and for the lines on which the issue was finally joined. Yet for chapters on the work of the antislavery agitators — work that began and ended with agitation — one finds scarcely a line devoted to the life-work of William Lowndes Yancey. An industrious biographer [1] has indeed published a mass of interesting facts about his life and times, but the book, though favorably known to investigators, has made little headway toward reëstablishing his fame. His very name, which in the later fifties was a rallying cry to the defenders of slavery, and

[1] John Witherspoon Du Bose.

to its assailants an execration, is known to few
who cannot go back in memory to those terrible
years.  Thousands of youth, fresh from the study
of their country's history even in our best colleges, would be astounded, no doubt, to hear a
claim advanced for him, as it might be, and quite
seriously, to a place among the half-dozen men
who have had most to do with shaping American
history in this century.  A pause over his grave
should not prove useless to those who are attempting a philosophical treatment of the period to
which he belongs.

He was of good Virginian ancestry, but his
father, Benjamin Cudworth Yancey, lived in
South Carolina, and was numbered with Lowndes,
Cheves, Calhoun, and Wilds, in the so-called
"legal galaxy" of the Palmetto State.  The father
died in 1817, when the son was three years old,
and left but a small fortune ; the boy's education
was therefore limited to a single year at Williams
College.  After that, he studied law at Green-
ville, South Carolina, and at twenty he was a prac-
titioner at the bar, the editor of a Unionist paper,
and an anti-nullification orator.  At twenty-one,
he married a wealthy lady and became a planter.
A year later, he went with his slaves to Alabama

and established himself at Oakland, a plantation
in the heart of the Black Belt, near Cahawba, the
first capital of the young commonwealth, — a city
of sudden birth and swift decay, now quite vanished from the earth.

Here he lived the quiet life of a cotton
planter until an irretrievable disaster, the accidental poisoning of his slaves, drove him back
into law and journalism ; and journalism and the
law led him into politics. Meanwhile, the headship of a slave establishment had so strengthened
the ties which bound him to his class and his
section that no trace of Unionism was left in
his mind when he entered the campaign of 1840
as a Van Buren man. Alabama was Democratic,
but the Whigs were making a wonderful canvass.
The demand for state rights oratory was great, and
it was as a state rights Democrat of the strictest
sect that Yancey first appeared, in the hard-cider
year, before Alabama audiences. His success was
such that for twenty years thereafter his sway over
the people of the state was comparable to nothing
that we of a cooler-headed generation have ever
seen. Chief Justice Stone, a jurist not unknown
to lawyers of the present day, once said : "I
first heard Mr. Yancey in 1840. I thought then,

and I yet think, he was the greatest orator I ever heard."

He rose rapidly to power. At twenty-seven, he was in the lower house of the legislature. At twenty-nine, he was a state senator. At thirty, a by-election sent him to Congress. His reputation as an orator had preceded him, and his first speech at Washington extended it widely, while the immediate consequences of the speech made him for a time a national celebrity. Clingman, of North Carolina, had become a target for Southern invective when he opposed the annexation of Texas, the principal measure under debate during the winter of 1844–45. To Yancey, though a new member, his fellows granted the distinguished privilege of replying for them all; and if he excelled in one sort of oratory more than another it was in impassioned invective. His speech made a pronounced impression on the House and the country, and Clingman, stung to the quick, demanded an explanation of certain personal allusions. Yancey haughtily declined to explain. Clingman then asked for "the satisfaction usual among gentlemen"; and with this demand his opponent, who had killed his man in an earlier affair, instantly complied.

The meeting was bloodless, and the opponents of dueling failed entirely in their efforts to make an example of the principals. Preston King's resolution for an investigation was beaten in the House, and the legislature of Alabama passed, over the governor's veto, an act relieving Yancey of the political disabilities which, under the laws of the state, he had incurred. To the *Alabama Baptist*, a religious paper which severely censured his course, Yancey wrote: " The laws of God, the laws of my own state, the solemn obligations due 'that young wife, the mother of my children,' to whom you so feelingly and chastely allude, were all considered ; but all yielded, as they have ever done from the earliest times to the present, to those laws which public opinion has framed, and which no one, however exalted his station, violates with impunity." It was a poor defence, but Alexander Hamilton's was little better.

Unopposed by the Whigs, Yancey was returned for the term beginning in 1845, and his reputation was much strengthened by his speeches during the first session. Apparently, he had every reason to look forward to a brilliant career in public life. But at the end of the session he resigned his seat, formed a partnership with a distinguished lawyer of Montgomery, and stated with the utmost clearness his reasons for retiring. He never again held office under the government of the United States. I have set down the facts of his career up to this point as briefly as I could, for the reason that his true life-work began with his withdrawal from Congress.

The address to his constituents in which he announced his retirement was in the main a bitter arraignment of the Northern Democrats. He charged them with subserviency to sectional interests antagonistic to the welfare of the South, and with infidelity to the party's historical principles. "If principle," he declared, "is dearer than mere party association, we will never again meet in common Democratic convention a large body of men who have vigorously opposed us on principle." The scorn of compromise was the key-note of his address; resistance to compromise was the sum total of the endeavor to which he thus committed himself. The recreant party must be brought back to the principles of strict construction or no longer leaned upon as the bulwark of Southern rights. The South must cease to rely on party, and insist, regardless of party platforms and party interests, upon all it had a

right to claim under the "compact of union."
The ultimate remedy for Northern aggression he
did not yet name; but when occasion arose, in
the controversy over the territory acquired from
Mexico, he named it promptly and clearly. It
was not nullification, or interposition, or any other
form of resistance inside the Union; it was secession from the Union. To the fight against compromise Yancey gave the remainder of his life. To
understand how he fought and why he won, it is
necessary to have some knowledge of the people
among whom he lived and the means of agitation
that were available.

Politically, the people of the Cotton states were
divided into three parties. There were, indeed,
few who did not call themselves either Whigs or
Democrats; but the extreme state rights men,
though they usually coöperated with the Democrats, repeatedly asserted themselves in such a
way as to present the aspect of a third party.
Although a majority of the great planters were
probably Whigs in name, they usually stood for
the interests of their class, and in consequence
they frequently found themselves in closer accord
with the state rights or " Southern Rights " Democrats of their own section than with the Whigs of

the North.   On the other hand, the bulk of the Democrats, small farmers, tradesmen, and the like were nowhere committed, except in South Carolina, to the extreme doctrines of Calhoun and other leaders in the resistance to centralization. There is no good reason to believe that either nullification or secession, considered as a policy, had a majority of the party in any state except South Carolina; and in South Carolina the Calhoun men controlled so completely that the ordinary party divisions can hardly be said to have prevailed there at all.   It was to the state rights men, mingled as they were with the supporters of both the great national parties, that Yancey turned for help in the task he had undertaken.

It may be said, however, that the public mind of the entire South was in a state altogether favorable to revolutionary enterprises.   A growing unrest was in many ways apparent.   Industrial unrest, due to economic causes, was exhibited in a revival of the migratory impulse.   Early in the fifties, we find Senator C. C. Clay complaining bitterly of the abandonment of lands near his home in the fertile valley of the Tennessee.   Olmsted's books are full of allusions to the westward movement of cotton growers, even from regions so recently settled as the valleys of the Alabama and Tombigbee rivers. It was about this time that the failure of the state bank systems throughout the South was finally accepted by the legislatures and the people. The political signs of unrest were unmistakable. In Yancey's own state, party lines were drawn in so many ways during the decade from 1845 to 1855 that the party names are bewildering. Whigs and Democrats, Bank men and Anti-Bank men, Unionists and Southern Rights men, Know-nothings and Anti-Know-nothings sought the favor of the people. At such a time, tenacity of purpose counted. In the midst of hesitation and indecision, Yancey had the immense advantage of knowing his own mind.

He had another advantage in that he lived among a people peculiarly incapable of resisting any appeal that might be made to them as his was, — a people over whom the power of a real orator was incalculable. An editor like Garrison, a poet like Whittier or Lowell, a novelist like Mrs. Stowe, could hardly have swayed the planters of Alabama as they swayed the people of New England; for it must be said of the lower South that its culture was not of books. Mr. Rhodes, guided by the testimony of European travellers,

has reached the conclusion that the best society
in the South was finer than in the North. "The
palm," he declares, "must be awarded to the slaveholding section." But the qualities that made the
Southern host so attractive to the travelled Englishman or Frenchman were not developed in an
atmosphere of free libraries or free public schools.
There were really no public libraries in the Cotton
states, and the public school system did not flourish
in a region so sparsely settled and so devoted to
agriculture. The literary activity which gave to the
world such new names as Hawthorne and Emerson
had in no wise stirred the lower South. Certain
newspapers, like those of Charleston and New
Orleans and the *Montgomery Advertiser*, were
edited with ability, and were by no means unimportant forces in politics. Indeed, if one gives
due weight to the fewness of cities, the influence
of the newspaper press seems to have been
fully as great as one could expect. But it was
the spoken word, not the printed page, that
guided thought, aroused enthusiasm, made history. It is doubtful if there ever has been a
society in which the orator counted for more
than he did in the Cotton Kingdom.

Yet at first blush it would seem that, as com-

pared with the lyceum orator of New England,
the oratorical agitator in the lower South had
serious obstacles to contend with. He had,
indeed, no such machinery as the lyceum to
bring him before his audiences. Moreover, the
railroads were few and short ; there were no
great cities and few important towns. But he
did not need the device of the lyceum to get an
audience. Its place was amply filled by the law
courts, the political meetings and conventions,
the camp-meetings, and the barbecues. For,
from the nature of their chief industry, the
people were unemployed during certain seasons ;
and they were all familiar with the uses of
horseflesh. Time was often heavy on their hands,
and everybody rode and drove. The cross-roads
church stood often quite out of sight of human
habitations, but its pews were apt to be well
filled on Sunday, and the branches of the trees
in front of it were worn with bridles. The
court-house, marking the county seat, might have
no other neighbors than a "general" store and
a wretched inn ; but when some famous lawyer
rose to defend a notorious criminal, hundreds,
even thousands, followed with flashing or tearful
eyes the dramatic action which surely accom-

panied his appeal. An important convention
was not without a "gallery" because it was
held in a town of few inhabitants and the mean-
est hotel accommodations. As to the barbecues
and camp-meetings, they were nothing less than
outpourings of the people. At Indian Springs,
in Georgia, during the hard-cider campaign, there
was given a barbecue to which "the whole
people of all Georgia" were invited. It was
attended by thousands; the orators, of whom
Yancey was one, spoke by day and by night; and
it lasted a week.

These, in fact, were the true universities of
the lower South, — the law courts, and the great
religious and political gatherings; as truly as a
grove was the university of Athens, or a church,
with its sculpture and paintings, the Bible of a
mediæval town. The man who wished to lead
or to teach must be able to speak. He could
not touch the artistic sense of the people with
pictures or statues or verses or plays; he must
charm them with voice and gesture. There
could be no hiding of the personality, no burying of the man in his art or his mission. The
powerful man was above all a person; his power
was himself. How such a great man mounted

the rostrum, with what demeanor he endured
an interruption, with what gesture he silenced
a murmur, — such things were remembered and
talked about when his reasoning was perhaps
forgotten.

Nor can it be said that the convictions thus
implanted were less deep and lasting than if they
had resulted, as in other communities, from
appeals addressed more especially to the intellect. The peculiarly impressionable character of
Southern audiences of that day, their quick
responsiveness to any plea that graced itself
with the devices of the one art they loved,
might very well have led a cool-headed observer
to measure the outcome by the criterion of
Latin-American civilization. Instability, lightness,
might with reason have been attributed to such a
people. But whatever changes had come over the
temper of the English stock in the Cotton states,
it had never lost its habit of fidelity to the cause
once espoused, its sternly practical way of turning words into deeds. What many a Northern
optimist considered mere bluster in the fifties
took on the horrid front of war in the sixties;
what seemed credulity in the farmer audiences
who merely listened and shouted rose into the

dignity of faith in the Petersburg trenches. He who cannot reconcile excitability with strength of purpose can never understand the people to whom Yancey spoke.[1]

Nowhere were these characteristics of the men of the lower South more strongly marked than in Yancey's own home and the region of which it was the centre. The country wagons that always filled the main square of the Alabama capital brought every day the two most forcible illustrations of his contention. The cotton bale was his object-lesson when he sought to quicken his people's sense of the interests which were endangered when the manufacturing states controlled at Washington. The negro on top of it was a constant reminder of mastery, a constant incitement to a heightened appreciation of the liberty that was still, as in Burke's day, not only an enjoyment, but a kind of rank and

---

[1] Even so perspicacious a Northern man as Lowell, on the very eve of the election in 1860, was assuring his countrymen that the Union was not in danger. " Mr. W. L. Yancey, to be sure, threatens to secede ; but the country can get along without him, and we wish him a prosperous career in foreign parts. . . . That gentleman's throwing a solitary somerset will hardly turn the continent head over heels." How grimly history glozes that ridicule !

privilege. To the Southerner, liberty meant nothing less than the right of himself and his community to be free from all interference by the peculiar outside world which had neither cotton nor slaves, — the meddlesome outside world which kept prating of a higher law, above the Constitution, above the Scriptures, rolling its *r*'s the while in such a disagreeable way.

It was not, however, after the fashion of the common demagogue that Yancey sought to lead his people. His claim to our respect as a political thinker is far stronger than that. He did not show them merely the obvious aspects of the sectional controversy. On the contrary, it is doubtful if any mind in the country dwelt more fixedly than his on the relations of the South to the rest of the Union, and of slavery to American civilization; or if any more remorselessly pursued the facts, from one point of view, to their remoter consequences and significance. In this regard, Yancey was no unworthy successor to Calhoun. He was never clamorous or shrill, however vehement he grew, because no particular exigency ever drew his attention from the main question. Perceiving from the outset that the crucial test of strength between slavery and its assailants must come in dealing with the territories, he took his stand on that question, and never changed it.

His first effort was to bring his party to his position ; and his position was first clearly stated in a political document once famous as the "Alabama platform" of 1848. To the Alabama Democratic convention of that year, called to choose delegates to the national convention, Yancey went as a delegate, carrying this document in his pocket. The committee on resolutions brought in a much milder declaration, but by a notable oratorical triumph he got his own views adopted instead. Following the line of Calhoun's resolutions of 1847, the platform declared that it was the duty of Congress not merely to permit slavery in the territories acquired from Mexico, but to protect it there. The most important clause was a denunciation of the new theory of squatter sovereignty, — a theory which Yancey always regarded as the most insidious of all attacks on the equality of the Southern states in the Union. The resolution on this doctrine became the true gospel of the fire-eaters. It read as follows : —

"*Resolved*, That the opinion advanced or maintained by some that the people of a territory acquired by the common toil, suffering, blood, and treasure of the people of all the states can, in other event than the forming of a state constitution, preparatory to admittance as a state in the Union, lawfully or constitutionally prevent any citizen of any such state from removing to or settling in such territory with his property, be it slave property or other, is a restriction as indefensible in principle as if such restriction were imposed by Congress."

The delegates pledged themselves to support no candidate for the presidency who would not openly oppose both methods of excluding slavery from the territories — by the action of Congress, and by the action of territorial legislatures. The delegates to the national convention at Baltimore, with Yancey at their head, were instructed to act in accordance with the resolutions. With Democrats elsewhere who would not accept the resolutions as good party doctrine the Alabama Democrats would have no fellowship. Yancey immediately wrote to the various aspirants for the presidential nomination for an expression of their views, in order that he and his associates might be governed by their replies.

This was the most advanced stand that any
party convention had yet taken in the controversy;
but for a moment it looked as if the whole of
the Southern democracy were going to take it at
once. The Alabama platform had done for the
proslavery agitation what the Virginia and Kentucky resolutions, at the close of the eighteenth
century, did for the Anti-Federalist impulse.
Democratic conventions in Florida and Virginia
hastened to adopt it; the legislatures of Georgia
and Alabama indorsed it. Then suddenly it fell
into disfavor. Moderate men who loved the
Union saw in it danger to the country's peace;
politicians, looking forward to the campaign,
scented danger to the party. Yancey returned
from a circuit of the courts to find the newspapers turning against him, the presidential
aspirants replying evasively to his letters, and
even his fellow-delegates wavering. He himself
did not waver for an instant. At Baltimore, he
spoke firmly, first objecting to the nomination
of a candidate until a platform should be agreed
on, and then urging his views in a minority
report from the committee on resolutions. His
amendment being rejected, and Cass, the reputed
author of the squatter sovereignty doctrine, being

named as the candidate, he arose, and with a single follower left the hall.

The situation when he returned to his home was an admirable one to try the temper of an agitator. The people crowded to hear him defend his course; at one meeting after another the Democrats urged him in affectionate terms to reconsider his purpose and yield to the will of the majority. But he had the born agitator's inability to accept defeat. He declined to support Cass, or in any way to recede from his position. On the contrary, he denounced with the utmost bitterness the course of his fellow-delegates at Baltimore. He would come back into the party when it abandoned squatter sovereignty, and not before. Alabama cast her electoral votes for Cass and Butler, and his labors seemed to have gone for nothing. He had failed in his attempt at party leadership. But one thing was left to him : his prestige as an orator always sufficed to get him a hearing. On one occasion, a public meeting first voted that he should not be heard, and then, when it was announced that he would speak on the other side of the street, adjourned thither *en masse* without the formality of a vote.

He kept on speaking, and before long the crisis of 1849–50 gave him another opening. As the time for the decision of the territorial question approached, party lines in the Cotton states grew weaker and weaker. Democrats who feared for the Union favored a compromise; many Whigs, moved by their attachment to slavery and the plantation system, favored a firm stand for the Southern contention. Yancey found himself in the forefront of the opposition to Clay's plan for saving the Union. He believed that the rights of the Southern states had been sacrificed in the compromise of 1820. To accept another arrangement that would hinder the extension of slavery was to his mind like submitting to a second branding. The honor of the South was at stake, not its material interests alone. With this appeal he won many to his side; it played upon the instinct that had kept the duello alive. He even found his way back into the councils of the Democratic party. That party, in fact, seemed on the eve of disruption throughout the South. Union men and Southern Rights men were struggling for the mastery in the organization. The people were really dividing, with little regard to parties, on the issue of compromise or resistance, and the Whigs were for the most part joining the Union Democrats. For the first time, there was a clear division in Yancey's own state between those who thought the plantation system safe inside the Union and those who were ready to weigh the peculiar interests and the honor of the South against the value of the Union.

In consequence, Yancey came face to face with men who opposed his leadership not because it endangered the welfare of a party, but because his ideas were a menace to the Union and they loved it. The defence of compromise, which in that exigency was the defence of the Union, was undertaken by men of no ordinary ability. In Alabama, Henry W. Hilliard, a Whig of national reputation in those days, and an orator hardly second to Yancey himself in effectiveness with popular audiences, was the Union leader. Senator William R. King, who was soon to die while the Vice-President's seat awaited him, counselled moderation and loyalty. Collier, the governor, Watts, who was to be governor and a member of the Confederate cabinet, Houston, who after many years was to lead his people out of the horrors of reconstruction, — were all firm Unionists. It was men like these in Alabama and the neighboring states who kept the Nashville convention from doing any mischief. It was they who gave Yancey, now at the head of the Southern Rights party, his second defeat. Their fight drew eloquent praise from Rufus Choate at the time, but nowadays it is hardly remembered that there ever was any fight for the Union in the lower South. They were successful in most of the congressional districts, and the party of resistance practically disappeared. But Yancey, with a corporal's guard of followers, refused to leave the field. In 1852, a national ticket, Troup and Quitman, was actually nominated and supported by a few thousands who stood in the South, as a like handful of steadfast abolitionists did in the North, for the view that the inevitable conflict was at hand. Yancey, in fact, never considered any other provocation comparable to the measures of 1850. In 1860, he declared that if he went out of the Union because of "a Black Republican victory," he would go "in the wake of an inferior issue"; the true justification for such action, in his mind, was that the Union had been destroyed ten years before, when the Southern states were denied equality

with the free states of the North in the common
territorial possessions.

But it was clear that the secessionists were
in a minority. Yancey had failed as the leader
of a separate party movement, as he had failed
before to win leadership in the old party. He and
his associates in the South were in like case with
Garrison and other extremists in the North.
His power waned again, but his fame was constantly growing. It did not proceed from above
downward, like the oratorical reputations of the
office-holders at Washington, but spread in an
ever widening circle among the people themselves,
until it pervaded states where his voice had not
yet been heard. His figure was now distinct and
threatening far beyond the limits of his immediate
personal influence. He had become the orator
of secession, the storm centre of Southern dis-
contents. More than that, he had made himself
feared by moderate men everywhere as the arch-
enemy of compromise. Now that Clay was dead,
Stephen A. Douglas had succeeded to the leadership of those who trusted Clay's devices. In
Douglas, and Northern men like him, Yancey saw
the constant obstacle in his path to leadership in
the South, for it was they who were forever be-

guiling the South with bargains and promises.
Douglas, on the other hand, might well have
studied, during the truce that followed the battle
of 1850, the man who, far more than any Northern rival, threatened him with defeat alike in his
policy and in his ambition.

But for the moment Douglas was having his
way. His doctrine of squatter sovereignty had
triumphed in the compromise, and he proceeded
now to extend it into new fields. The passage
of the Kansas-Nebraska Bill in 1854 marked the
lowest ebb in Yancey's political fortunes. It
seemed to prove what his opponents at home
had all along contended, — that slavery was safe
in the Union; for was not the whole great West
thrown open to the master and the slave? In
vain he warned his people against the delusive
concession. His was no patient spirit, but he was
compelled to wait for events to prove that Douglas
was not the saviour of the South.

Events, however, were moving rapidly. The extremists of the North were helping the extremist
leaders in the South. The Free-soilers of Kansas were working for them; John Brown was their
ally. For a moment, indeed, Yancey seems to
have been misled by the Cincinnati platform of

1856, and by Buchanan's adroitly worded letter
of acceptance, into the belief that his triumph was
coming in the form in which he had sought it at
Baltimore, — within the lines of the party ; for,
apparently thinking that the party had discarded
the Douglas doctrine when it rejected Douglas
as a candidate, he went into the Alabama convention, regained his party standing, and supported
Buchanan.   But the party persisted with the
Douglas policy in Kansas, and with the failure
of the scheme Yancey saw the approach of his
real triumph, — a triumph that should crush
Douglas, who for a time had made him powerless, overthrow the time-servers in his party, who
had twice overthrown him, and bring to his feet
his own people, who had twice refused to follow
him.

The vision made him more impatient than
ever.   He devoted himself to the ways and means
of hastening the consummation.   In Southern
commercial conventions he insisted with arrogance
on the separateness of the South's industrial interests.   He even denounced as unconstitutional
the laws forbidding the foreign slave-trade, supporting his position with the most extraordinary
reasoning in the history of constitutional inter-

pretations. Finally, in 1858, he wrote, and after-
ward defended, a note to a correspondent which
found its way into print and became known far
and wide as the " scarlet letter." " No national
party can save us," he declared ; "no sectional
party can save us. But if we could do as our
fathers did — organize committees of safety all
over the Cotton states (and it is only in them that
we can look for any effective movement) — we
shall [*sic*] fire the Southern heart, instruct the
Southern mind, give confidence to each other, and
at the proper moment, by one organized concerted
action, we can precipitate the Cotton states into
revolution."

The Democrats of Alabama, now united on the
platform of 1848, to which even the moderate men
had been driven by the outcome of the squatter
sovereignty experiment, sent Yancey to the national convention at Charleston with practically
the same message he had carried to Baltimore.
About the same time, the legislature instructed
the governor to call a convention of the people
of the state in the event of the election of a
" Black Republican " to the presidency. Yancey
went to Charleston assured that the whole lower
South was behind him. Douglas, still pursuing

his great ambition, saw his fate in Yancey's hands, and went as far to meet the fire-eaters as he could go without abandoning all hope of an effective support in the North.

But the men of the Cotton states, knowing that their hour was come, would accept nothing less than the whole of that for which they had so long contended. When once again, after twelve years of defeat and exile, Yancey rose to speak before a national convention, he had such an opportunity as rarely comes even to an American orator. The imperious tones of his wonderful voice fell with strange power on the assembly. The trembling delegates hung upon his words, for they saw in his hands the fate, not of Douglas alone, but of the party, perhaps of the Union. If to grant his demands was party suicide, it was hardly less party suicide to refuse them. By a few votes, the Southern platform was rejected. He left the hall, and now, not the single follower of twelve years before, but the delegates of seven states, trooped at his heels. In the end, yet others followed.

When Douglas, finally receiving the nomination of those who remained, went before the people, he found Yancey awaiting him. Declining the

offer of the vice-presidency from the friends of
Douglas, Yancey had joined the seceders at Baltimore, where he favored the nomination of Breck-
inridge on the extreme Southern platform, and
then entered on a canvass of the Northern states :
a *tour de force* that smacks either of overfed ambition or else of a real hope that there might be
such a union as he had always held the Constitution to define, — a union in which the will of
the majority should count for nothing against
the letter of the Constitution as he read it. He
spoke in the Middle states, in New England,
and in the West. He even spoke in Faneuil
Hall, and silenced a threatening uproar where
Phillips had conquered his first mob. His attitude toward his Northern audiences is perhaps
best exhibited in his last speech on Northern
soil, made when the result of the election was
already clearly foreshadowed.

"My countrymen," he said at Cincinnati, "you
cannot carry out the policy of the Black Republican party. You cannot carry it out, and expect
the South to remain submissively bowing down
to your supremacy. We are for the Union.
What union ? For the union, gentlemen, contained between these two lids" (holding up the

Constitution). ". . . Can you obtain anything, gentlemen, by destroying, even if you are able, my section, save the memory of a great wrong that would haunt you through eternity? . . . But do not, do not, my friends of the North, — I say it before you in no spirit, gentlemen, of servile submission to your power, or of servile acknowledgment of that power, for as God rules I have no fear of it, as much as I respect it, — but do not, merely because you have the power, do not wreathe your arms around the pillars of our liberty, and, like a blind Samson, pull down that great temple on your heads as well as ours."

From the time he crossed the Ohio, his journey homeward was like a triumphal progress. At Nashville, the horses were taken from his carriage and his admirers drew it through the streets. At New Orleans, an informal holiday was proclaimed, that all might hear him. When he reached Montgomery, he found Douglas just leaving the city; that night, no hall could contain the multitudes thronging to hear their champion, whom they hailed as the foremost orator of the world. At last they were ready to follow where he led. The lower South voted for the candidate of his choice, and the day after the election lifelong opponents of his policy joined their voices to his and advocated the final step into disunion.

But his triumph was not to be completed without a struggle. The friends of the Union in his own state were driven to the wall, but they made one more gallant fight before they yielded. They were still strong in northern Alabama, and with them were joined some who, seeing secession inevitable, were yet disposed to wait until coöperation with other states could be assured, and others, no doubt, who were stirred by no higher motive than a sullen unwillingness to accept a leadership so long rejected. The temper of the convention was in doubt until it assembled, and on the first test vote the majority for immediate secession was but eight. The spirited opposition roused Yancey into an arrogance which the Union leaders, who were wanting neither in ability nor in courage, answered with sturdy defiance. Defeated, however, in their attempt to get the ordinance submitted to the people, they for the most part yielded, in the hope that unanimity might give strength to the movement they deprecated; but no less than twenty-four refused to sign the instrument. The results of submitting the ordinance to the people in Texas, and later in Virginia, give us no reason to believe that the decision of Alabama could have been changed.

Yancey's desire was history. Suddenly, and as if by some enchantment, the Cotton Kingdom had risen to face the world. Before his eyes, in his own home, he saw a new government established, a new flag unfurled. It was fit, indeed, that his should be the voice to welcome Jefferson Davis when he came to take his place at the head of the new Confederacy, for no other single voice had availed so much to call it into existence. But his work was done. He soon sailed away to Europe at the head of the commission sent to secure recognition for the Confederacy among the great powers. Returning from that bootless mission, he took his seat in the Confederate Senate, and in the turbulent debates of that gloomy and impotent legislature, his last energies were consumed. A painful malady had long sapped his strength, and in the summer of 1863 he went home to die. In the delirium of fever his voice sometimes rose in fierce commands to visionary hosts on unseen battlefields. But his passing was little marked.

The orators had given place to the captains. His people were working out in blood and fire the destiny up to which he had led them.

I shall not attempt an estimate of this career. There is the same doubt of its importance which attaches always to the career of a forerunner. Events would perhaps have taken the same course without him, and the silent forces would have worked out the inevitable if he had never raised his voice. Moreover, his was but one, though the clearest and firmest, of many eloquent voices. But surely it is too important a career to be neglected by those who write our history. Yet our knowledge of the man is almost entirely matter of tradition. He wrote no books, and published no collection of his speeches. The fragments that remain bear the marks of imperfect reporting, for the most effective of his addresses were those delivered before popular audiences, usually in the open air, and they were not taken down. What is left could never be treated as literature, and conveys, indeed, but a vague notion of his oratory. Yet there are paragraphs which, read with the single purpose to estimate their immediate effect on those who heard them, and with due regard to time and place,

impress one very strongly with his mastery of
the instrument he used. The sentences sometimes rush like charging cavalry. There are
phrases that ring out like bugle calls. It is the
language of passionate purpose ; of an orator bent
on rousing, convincing, overwhelming the men in
front of him, not on meeting the requirements
of any standard of public speech.

Of his look and bearing we have better record,
for it is of these things that Southern tradition
is most careful. He had little of the *poseur* about
him ; what most impressed men was his grim
fixedness of purpose. He was not given to fran-
tic gesticulation, and it is said that he rarely occupied more than a square yard of space even in
his longest speeches. His chief physical endow-
ment was his voice, — "the most perfect voice,"
one tells us, "that ever aroused a friendly audience
to enthusiasm or curbed to silence the tumults of
the most inimical." A youth who heard it years
ago, and who, since then, in the course of a long
career in Congress and in the Cabinet, has doubtless encountered all the notable orators of his
time, declares it was "sweeter, clearer, and of
more wonderful compass and flexibility" than any
other he ever heard. In personal appearance,

though handsome, he was in no wise extraordinary. There was even a lack of animation in his ordinary aspect in his later years, and a look of nervous exhaustion. The mastery and pride of his face in the portrait in the state-house at Montgomery is sufficiently exceptional even there to draw upon the ill-painted canvas the eye that wanders among the unremembered governors and judges of his time. But oratory, we know, is action, and the truer likeness of the man is the image of tremendous articulate passion which abides in the minds of those who fell under his power half a century ago.

There is so much about Yancey to suggest a comparison with Wendell Phillips that I have been constantly tempted to set the two side by side in my thought. Their names, indeed, were often coupled in the invective of the moderate men of those days : Yancey the " fire-eater," and Phillips the " abolitionist fanatic." Their careers stand out in striking similarity and in equally striking contrast. The similarity lay chiefly in their mental characteristics and methods of work ; the contrast was in the causes for which they stood, and the fates they met.

It is easy to think of them as the Luther and the St. Ignatius of the revolt against slavery. But Yancey's spiritual kinship was not wholly with the Spaniard: in him, no less than in Phillips, there was something of the German's temper. The two extremists were alike in their relentless hostility to every form of compromise, to every disguise with which men sought to conceal the sterner aspect of affairs. If both were enthusiasts, neither was a mere dreamer. The fever in their blood brought them, not fanciful visions, but a keener insight into the disorder of the body politic than was given to more sluggish natures. The oratory of both was simple and direct, because both saw and purposed clearly. Both were appealing from the politicians to the people, and they spoke a language which the people understood, however the politicians marvelled. Both, I sometimes think, were wiser than their contemporaries who were judging the situation by the standard of the ordinary, because both were alive to the imminence of an extraordinary crisis.

But here the likeness ends and the contrast begins. The heroism which one displayed for a moral principle the other devoted to a political purpose. One fortified himself with an appeal to a higher law, the other with the compromises of the Constitution. One looked to the future for his justification, the other demanded of the future that it break not with the past. Standing thus for causes as opposite as the poles, they encountered destinies as diverse: one, a success that proved the beginning of utter failure; the other, defeats that are forgotten in his dateless triumph.

For the surprising and neglected fact of the outcome is that Yancey really led his people in the way he chose, while Phillips never marked out the path along which the Republic was finally to march to the heights of his ideal. Not one specific design of the abolitionist extremists was ever accomplished in the way they planned: neither the breaking away of New England, nor the rising of the slaves under John Brown, nor any interference by Congress with slavery in the states. But in the end freedom prevailed. Yancey's definite purpose was to erect a Southern Confederacy, and he died under its flag. Yet to-day his Confederacy is a vanished dream, and he himself, within the lives of men who saw his beginning and ending, little more than a tradition.

The traveller in New England, well acquainted

with the just fame of the great abolitionist, is surprised to find among his surviving contemporaries an inadequate appreciation of his genius. The traveller in the lower South is equally astonished to find that a man whose name he has scarcely heard is honored there as the first orator of the century. On the gravestone of this forgotten orator it is recorded that he was "justified in all his deeds"; yet all about his grave there are so many graves of simple and honorable gentlemen who gave their lives and fortunes to the dreadful task he set them that one can fancy even his proud spirit crying out to be delivered from the body of that death. Nevertheless, the generous people who followed him have not condemned him; nor may we, since he was an orator, deny him refuge in the defence of Demosthenes: "Lay not the blame on me, if it was Philip's fortune to win the battle; the end depended on the will of God, and not on me."

# III.  THE RESOURCES OF THE CONFEDERACY

# III

# THE RESOURCES OF THE CON-
# FEDERACY

IN one of Mr. W. E. Henley's hospital poems, a sailor, "set at euchre on his elbow," tells in twenty lines what he saw from the wharf at Charleston when he was there off a blockade runner near the end of the American Civil War. Professor John C. Schwab, of Yale, after long and patient investigation of many obscure sources, has written a financial and industrial history of the South during the war which exhibits every characteristic of the most painstaking school of economic historians. His paragraphs are so meaty with facts, his references so abundant, his method so consistently scientific, his work, in a word, is so thoroughly well done, that it is hard to see how industry and intelligence could have gone farther.

Yet it is a question whether "The Confederate States of America" or Mr. Henley's verses will prove the more serviceable to the ordinary reader, trying to get a notion of what was inside the shell

that crackled to pieces before the great armies of
Grant and Sherman. Such is the complexity of
civilized societies, so many and so artificial are the
forms which the ordinary processes of production
and distribution, buying and selling, borrowing
and lending, come to take, so constantly does the
play of human motives disarrange the machinery
of industry and government, so wide a margin of
error must the student allow in his observations,
that failure in one sense is always predicable of
an enterprise like Professor Schwab's. The work
will of necessity be incomplete, for to reconstruct
a civilization by setting one stone upon another
is beyond the industry of a lifetime; and it will
not be rounded out by the reader himself, it is not
supplemented by his sympathetic understanding,
it does not stimulate his imagination. The difference between Professor Schwab's treatment of
the dead Confederacy and what a poet, a novelist,
a literary historian, might do with it, is like the
difference between an artist's and an anatomist's
treatment of a human body. We do not judge
the artist's work by the number or even by the
truth of its details; its aim is to make us see
and understand the whole by virtue of a quality
common to us and it. On the anatomist or the

anatomist-historian our demand is different. His
work is unfinished until the last tissue of the
body or the body politic is dissected into its
minutest cells. Neither anatomy nor political
science can ever attain its object completely, as
painting and poetry do sometimes attain theirs.
Mr. Henley's sailor man might not more enlighten
us if his glimpse from the wharf were widened
into a vision of the whole harassed South. Professor Schwab's book will be the more valuable
for every correction which he may make in his
tables of prices and note-issues, for every newspaper file which he may in a future edition make
a footnote to refer us to.

But there is also a sense in which a work like
this may be complete, — a sense in which it may
very well pass completeness and tend to surfeit :
that is to say, if one has regard for the reader's
limitations. There is a point beyond which
the writer cannot go without disregarding the
"reader" altogether, not in the matter of his
mere interest and pleasure, but in the matter of
his attention and memory, of his ability to carry
a mass of facts in his head long enough to connect
them with what may follow. Of course, there
are readers and readers, but it should be no

harder to gauge the average mind in this than in many other of the respects in which one must gauge it in books and in life, and to stop short of the line beyond which, for the average mind, scarcely a single general principle or important relation of cause and effect will stand out through the haze to reward the effort which the reading of such a book requires.

Of course, too, it is not the " reader " but the student that books like this are meant for.  Yet the reader also has some claims.  There are questions which every intelligent person is moved to ask about the Confederacy, and here are the answers; but one may miss them altogether if the results of the investigation are set forth too abstrusely, or too cautiously, or too minutely. Professor Schwab and another scientist, Professor E. A. Smith, of Allegheny College, — who limits himself, however, to a study of the Confederate treasury, — come forward from their dissection of a defunct state, and we wish to know of them, not what discoveries or confirmations they have to report to their brother scientists, but what was the strength that sustained the Southern Confederacy while it lived, and what disease or wound or weakness it died of.  Perhaps it may be practicable to extract from their reports, restrained as they are, and resolutely void of gossip and conjecture, some satisfaction of our unenlightened curiosity.

Our question is not meant to cover the military struggle. With the main features of that, educated Americans — and many Englishmen as well, now that they have books like Colonel Henderson's "Stonewall Jackson" — are reasonably well acquainted. But it seems nowadays to be generally conceded that while the armies on both sides were composed almost entirely of volunteers, and so small that the North's superiority in wealth and numbers had not begun to tell, the South's advantages of fighting on interior lines and of possessing more good riders and good shots did tell heavily. It would perhaps be conceded also that the South had men enough, if she could have kept them in the field well armed and well clothed and well fed, to withstand even the vast numbers which the North did put in the field and liberally equip and sustain. We all understand, too, that after the first few months the blockade forced the Confederates to rely on their own resources far more nearly altogether than the Southern leaders in secession had apprehended. Were the available resources inadequate, or were they neglected or wasted? Why were the Southern armies always ill armed, ill clad, ill fed, ill paid? How far was the outcome, inevitable though it may have been, immediately attributable to faults and errors?

If we disregard the already accomplished effects of slavery on Southern industry, it was probably of advantage to the Confederates that the laborers in their fields were as a class less easily demoralized by war than a free white peasantry would have been. There is nothing to indicate that, until the country was overrun by Union troops, the blacks on the farms and plantations were less efficient than in peace. They made no move to rise. It was not found necessary to exempt from military service more than one owner or overseer for every twenty slaves, and the exemption did not keep more than five or six thousand men out of the army. Here was an agricultural labor system, defective, no doubt, but which did not need to be adapted to the emergency, and which, when it was diverted from cotton-growing — partly by the loss of the market for cotton, and partly by concerted purpose — was equal to the task of producing a food supply adequate to all wants, save that certain foods in common use, but not absolutely indispensable, could not be produced in the South at all.  For some of these, like tea and coffee, passable substitutes were contrived; the insufficiency of salt and of various medicines was the difficulty most nearly insuperable.  There was, besides, a good part of the four and a half million bales of cotton of the crop of 1860, the entire four millions of the crop of 1861, the million or more of 1862, the half million each of 1863 and 1864.  The South had sufficient food, and it had in abundance a principal raw material of clothing.  Tobacco was plentiful, — no mean item in war, as veterans both of the Civil War and of the Spanish War will testify.  Tanneries were commoner than any other sort of manufactories, and the supply of leather, though scant, could be eked out with various substitutes.  There were vast resources of timber, and all the raw material for making iron; contrary to the general notion, the great deposits of iron ore in northern Alabama were known before the war, and tentative attempts to exploit them had been made.

But it was simply impossible to build the furnaces and mills and railroads which were needed to make these resources fully effective.  The fact that the manufactories and railroads were not brought up to the requisite development is in itself the best of reasons for believing that they could not have been, with the labor and the capital that were available; for such manufactories as were set up, such railroads as were already built, — some of them were extended with government aid, — were extremely profitable. The motives of self-interest and patriotism, combined with the pressure of want and of military necessity, were not enough. A beginning was made on many lines, and in consequence there appeared for the first time in the Cotton states a strong sentiment for protection, and one heard it said that the blockade, like the old embargo and the second war with Great Britain, was going to prove a blessing. But four years of the most favorable conditions under peace would not have brought these industries near maturity. The machinery and the skilled labor could not be found under the actual conditions of a blockaded coast and an invaded border. The government itself, finding it impracticable to get all the small arms and ammunition it needed from abroad, made a headway which was on the whole remarkable toward supplying its wants at home; but the factories it established could not turn out small arms fast enough. The greater number came from United States arsenals seized at the outset, from captures in battle, and from abroad. In heavy ordnance, mainly through the work of the Tredegar Iron Works at Richmond, the domestic output was more considerable. President Davis, who had been in the old army, and Secretary of War in Pierce's Cabinet, could bring a valuable training and experience to the particular problem of arms and equipment, and his account of what was done with the means at hand shows that it was done intelligently and vigorously. We must admit the impossibility of so transforming the whole industrial system of the South as to meet the sudden demand for commodities which had never been produced there, and limit ourselves to the question whether the best use was made of what the Confederates could produce and of their opportunities to buy or borrow.

There was, first, the hope of aid from foreign countries, and of that cotton was naturally the basis. The situation was tantalizing. The price of cotton in England rose from the moment of separation, and it continued to rise until, when the blockade became effective, it reached a figure which would have enriched every planter in the

Confederacy if he could have marketed his product. Firms and individuals who took the risks of running cotton through the blockade grew rich, notwithstanding heavy losses. Foreign concerns adventured in it. The government went into it extensively through agencies like John Frazer & Co., of Charleston, by sharing the risks and profits of private enterprise, and by establishing a bureau and putting four steamers of its own in commission. At the end of 1863, Bullock, head of the secret service abroad, reported that thirty-one thousand bales had been shipped by the government from the two ports of Charleston and Wilmington to Liverpool. A separate bureau was established in Texas, and there was a lively trade in cotton and small arms across the Mexican line; but with the fall of Vicksburg the Federal mastery of the line of the Mississippi materially lessened the practical value of government assets in that quarter. The suggestion that the government might at the very outset have got possession of all the cotton in the country, shipped it abroad, made it a basis of credit with foreign governments and financiers, and grown rich with its rise in value, has often been made, but is readily dismissed. The government had not the means either to buy the cotton or to transport it.

After England, it is probable that the United States, of all "foreign countries," contributed the most, through trade, of the things which the Confederates were in pressing need of. Always forbidden, at first sincerely opposed, then winked at, and finally shared in by the Confederate government, trade through the lines was constantly proving the strength of the commercial impulse on both sides. Cotton and tobacco slipped out ; salt, bacon, and other commodities came in. President Lincoln had and exercised the authority to license individuals to trade with the Confederates. The government at Richmond actually speculated in the notes of the United States.

But one foreign loan was attempted, and of that also cotton was the basis. By a contract signed at Richmond in January, 1863, Erlanger & Cie., of Paris, underwrote at seventy-seven per cent of their face value Confederate bonds to the amount of three million pounds sterling. The interest was payable in specie, but the bonds were exchangeable at their face value for New Orleans middling cotton at sixpence a pound. That was little more than one-fourth the price of cotton abroad, and the

Erlangers made a pretty penny by their venture;
but the government, what with the agent's profits
and commissions, repurchases to affect the market,
and interest paid, got little more than half the face
value of the loan according to Professor Smith's
calculation, less than half according to the more
careful calculation of Professor Schwab. However,
its receipts were in specie, and far larger in proportion than it realized on any but the earliest of
its domestic loans. The single foreign loan was
clumsily managed, and it seems clear that a larger
one should have been tried. Possibly, the hope
of recognition restrained the government in the
matter, but it is reasonable to suppose that the
enlisting of great financial interests in England
and France would have been of more help toward
that end than the object lesson of a few securities
held up to prices in the European market which
compared favorably with the quotations of United
States bonds. However, barring some good fortune which might have raised up for the Confederacy a European ally to play a part comparable
to France's in the American Revolution, the
shrewdest diplomacy and financiering would not
have relieved it of the necessity to demand the
heaviest sacrifices of its devoted people. It could

not have drawn from without, either by trade or by borrowing, more than a small part of what it needed to keep its armies in the field.

The devotion of the Southerners was in fact immeasurable ; the economic agree with the military historians that their sacrifices were far greater than any the Revolutionary patriots made. The first revenues of the Confederate government were from voluntary loans of states and free gifts of individuals. The first requisition on the treasury was met with the personal credit of the Secretary. In the day of extreme need, women offered the hair of their heads to be sold abroad for arms.

A state of war enabled the government to get revenue by other extraordinary means than gifts and the loans of states. The United States customs receipts at Southern ports and the bullion in the New Orleans mint were taken before war was declared. A circular issued in March, 1861, directed that all dues to the United States government be paid into the Confederate treasury. A law of Congress passed in May provided that all debts due to citizens of the United States should likewise be paid into the treasury, and certificates given in exchange. The Washington government retaliated with a confiscation act, and in August a Confederate act sequestrated the property of all alien enemies, Confederate and state bonds exempted, and set apart the proceeds to reimburse citizens whose property had been taken by the United States. Pettigru, the foremost lawyer of South Carolina, attacked the law as unconstitutional ; but Judge Magrath, of the Confederate District Court, held that the power to pass it was a necessary attribute of such sovereignty as the Confederate government possessed — a position very like that which the United States Supreme Court came to in its last legal-tender decision. Late in 1864, the property of renegades and émigrés was confiscated. But the revenue from confiscations could not have been much above 6 millions, unless we include what the states got by like measures. It has been suggested that the entire debt of the South to the North at the beginning of the war, which is variously estimated, — Professor Schwab does not pretend to do more than conjecture that it was about 40 millions, — should be counted a Confederate asset, and the same sort of reasoning would make the stoppage of interest payments to Northerners on the bonds of Southern states and corporations an addition to the Southern resources. The list of extraordinary revenues

should certainly include the specie of the New Orleans banks, which was sent inward when the city
fell, and taken by the government, nominally as a
deposit. Nearly 5 millions were obtained that way.

There remained the two ordinary sources of
revenue, — taxation, and domestic loans. But the
first was curtailed by the blockade to such a
degree that the Confederate customs receipts may
best be grouped with the receipts from gifts and
confiscations, so trifling was the amount. One of
the earliest laws of the provisional Congress at
Montgomery imposed a duty of one-half of one
cent a pound on all exports of cotton, payable in
specie or in the coupons of the first issue of bonds,
the interest on which was guaranteed by the tax.
A month later, the first tariff law was passed, with
a long free list and a rate of fifteen per cent on a
few imports: it was thought advisable to put a
premium on immediate importations. A small
tonnage duty was for the sole purpose of main-
taining lighthouses. The permanent tariff passed
in May was of necessity a purely revenue measure,
for the provisional Constitution, like the permanent
one which followed, expressly forbade protection,
although both instruments omitted the prohibition
of export duties which is in the United States

Constitution — a matter of surprise to any one who recalls that thirty years earlier the nullifiers held the "tariff of abominations" to be virtually a tax on exports. The law followed the Walker principle of 1846, aiming to fix the minimum rates which would yield the maximum returns, made the rates *ad valorem* wherever practicable, — the highest twenty-five per cent, and the lowest five per cent, — and left the free list still long. For the first fiscal year, the receipts from import and export duties, seizures, and confiscations, all together, were less than $2\frac{1}{2}$ millions in specie.

So taxation, to be effective, must take its most direct and inquisitorial form, harassing to the taxpayers and laborious to the collectors. That the government should have been loath to adopt so unpopular a policy is not surprising; but that any government so driven upon it as that was should have delayed so long, and then resorted to it so timidly and tentatively, is explicable only on a low estimate of the Confederate lawmakers and of the Southern public opinion which their practice of secret sessions does not seem to have emboldened them to disregard. But the weakness of the government was more culpable than the outcry of the people. Years of prosperity and

peace under the Union had wonted them to light
burdens of taxation, and they were imbued with
hostility to the whole theory of a strong central
authority. They did, in fact, more nearly keep
pace with their government in recognizing the
necessity of heavy taxation than taxpayers often
do. At one time, a considerable body of public
opinion actually urged Congress on to its duty,
and the clamor against the laws when they were
passed was in large part due to the inequalities
they contained.

In July, 1861, Secretary Memminger estimated
at 4600 million dollars the assessable values in
real estate, slaves, and personal property, and
Congress, aiming to raise 25 millions, passed in
August a direct war tax of one-half of one per
cent on all property but government bonds
and money on hand, making the usual exemptions. The assessment, however, fell below the
Secretary's estimate by nearly 400 millions, and
as a matter of fact less than one-tenth of the
tax was ever collected from the taxpayers. It
was not apportioned among the states, for the
provisional Constitution made no such require-
ment ; but each state was a tax division, and could
obtain a rebate of ten per cent for its citizens by

paying the whole of their quota, less the rebate, before the date fixed for collections. The result was that all but one or two states borrowed the money. The total receipts from the "tax," some of them not covered in for a year or more, were less than 20 millions in a currency already much depreciated. The rate was too low, and the law ill-framed. The taxes which the Confederacy imposed during the first two years of the war were absurdly light in comparison with those ordinarily imposed by civilized states in time of peace.

The serious resort to taxation came at the beginning of the third year, and it was all the more unwelcome because it was belated. In April, 1863, the Congress passed a property tax of eight per cent, license taxes on various occupations, a graded income tax, a tax of ten per cent on the profits from sales of food-stuffs and a few other commodities, and a tax in kind, or tithe, on the products of agriculture. By this time, the area under control of the government was much diminished, and assessable values shrunken by many millions. The currency was depreciating so fast that it put a great premium on delay in payments. No collections were made until the end of the year, and by April, 1864, but 60 millions in currency, valued roughly at one-twentieth of that sum in specie, had been covered into the treasury. The next six months brought 42 millions in currency, or 2 millions in specie. The receipts from the tax in kind cannot be given in terms of money. Officially, the proceeds in 1863 were estimated at 5 millions in currency. The next year, there was gathered the equivalent of 30 million rations. Professor Smith estimates the total returns from the tithe at 145 millions in currency. The trouble and expense of collection were great, and so was the waste. In February, 1864, the tax law of 1863 was reënacted with higher rates on property, credits, and profits : the Secretary's estimate of assessable values at that time was 3 billions. In June, the rates were raised horizontally, and at the very end, in March, 1865, extreme rates were imposed.

The law was unconstitutional, for the permanent Constitution required all direct taxes to be apportioned among the states according to their representation in Congress. Certain states held it an infringement of their rights, more particularly because it taxed property which they had exempted and banks in which they had an interest. The tithe was the feature most bitterly resented, as inquisitorial, as imposing a special burden on agriculture, already depressed by the loss of its markets, and because the farmers could not profit by delay in payments, as everybody else could, but would lose by it instead. There were other inequalities. But the law, onerous as it was, did not bring the tax receipts up to a high place in the schedule of government revenues. The last full statement available, of October 1, 1864, for the six months preceding, shows that less than twelve per cent of the total receipts came from that source. The failure to tax promptly, to tax skilfully and equally, and to tax heavily, was a damning fault and weakness of the government. The rival government at Washington fell into the same error, but recovered from it in time.

The error is not to be measured by the inadequate tax receipts alone, but by the extent to which it impaired and vitiated the final device of borrowing. Had the government adhered to the sound policy it began with when it passed an export tax, payable in specie, to guarantee the interest on its first loan, it might have avoided — at least so long as by hook or by crook, at whatever cost, specie could be obtained — its unenviable preëminence among all modern governments as an exponent of forced loans and redundant note issues. Southern civilization, with sins enough to answer for already, might have escaped the crowning indictment that after centuries of money exchanges it brought Anglo-Saxon Americans back to plain barter in their market-places.

The first loan of 15 millions was negotiated on a specie basis, and it was successful. The Southern banks, holding perhaps 25 millions of specie, agreed to redeem in specie such of their notes as should be paid for the bonds, and for a year or two the interest, guaranteed by the export tax, was paid in specie. The second issue, in May, of 50 millions, was accompanied with no such guarantee of interest payments. Moreover, treasury notes to the amount of 20 millions were authorized by the same act, to be issued in lieu of bonds, and to be interchangeable with them. The loan was increased to 100 millions in August, and in December to 150 millions. The bonds were offered for specie, for military stores, and for the proceeds of the sale of raw produce or manufactured articles, so that the issue became largely a produce loan ; four hundred thousand bales of cotton, and tobacco and other farm products in proportion, were subscribed. The relief of the planters was an avowed object. Through this policy, the government came to number four hundred and fifty thousand bales of cotton, scattered over the country, among its assets. The receipts in money from sales of bonds during the first year were stated to be 31 millions, or twenty-two per cent of the total receipts.

The second year saw a great increase in the number of bonds authorized to be issued, but no corresponding increase in the sales. Of 165 millions authorized in April, $3\frac{1}{2}$ millions were placed. In September, the Secretary was empowered to sell bonds without limit to meet appropriations. But only nine per cent of the total receipts of the year came from that source. The third year, the receipts from bonds rose to twenty-two per cent of the total, and of the 1221 millions of debt accumulated by January 1, 1864, omitting the foreign loan, 298 millions were bonded. But the figures are misleading, for practically all the bond sales of the year, except those handled by the Erlangers, were in the nature of a half-compulsory funding. Similarly, the bond sales of the last year were nearly all accomplished through the compulsory funding act of February, 1864, which amounted to a repudiation of all treasury notes which should not be funded by certain dates. By the same act, six per cent bonds to the amount of 500 millions were authorized for current expenses, and the last full statement, of October 1, 1864, shows that but little over 14 millions of these had been sold. The debt was then 1371 millions, and 362 millions of it were funded, but less than half of the funded debt could be called voluntary loans. More than half the bonds had been sold by compulsion.

Of the enormous forced loan remaining, 178 millions were in interest-bearing notes and certificates, and 831 millions in notes bearing no interest. Beginning in March, 1861, with an issue of 1 million of treasury notes bearing interest, following that up in May with 20 millions of notes bearing no interest, the government had from the start paid the great bulk of its expenses with notes of the one class or the other. By the end of the first year, $105\frac{1}{2}$ millions had been issued; at the end of the second, the debt was $567\frac{1}{2}$ millions, and eighty-two per cent of it was in notes. In 1863, new issues more than counterbalanced the reduction accomplished by funding, and even the repudiation act of February, 1864, only temporarily diminished the rate of increase. That law required the holders of old notes, some of them fundable in eight per cent bonds, either to fund them in four per cent bonds or exchange them for new notes at the rate of three for two ; otherwise, they were to be taxed out of existence. Perhaps 300 millions were either funded or exchanged, but the remainder, though repudiated, continued to circulate. After October, 1864, current expenses were met mainly with treasury warrants and certificates of indebtedness, so that an immense floating debt was piled up ; but the expiring utterance of the Confederate Congress was another issue of notes, the bill passing over the veto of President Davis.

We may admit that the government could not have avoided forced loans and an inflated currency, even if it had made the wisest use of all other means of getting revenue. Ordinary standards of public finance cannot justly be applied to it. But it is hard to see how it could have chosen a worse policy than it did. To issue notes in quantities vastly beyond the demands of business, to repudiate them, and then to go on issuing more, must be near the height of bad finance. To show the effects of the policy completely, it would be necessary to examine every department of indus-

try and trade — a study of great interest to econ-
omists. Here, it is sufficient to point out that the
redundant paper currency was the main cause of
the government's failure to get the most possible
out of the material resources and productive industries of the South.

It was intended that the notes should take the
place of the old United States currency. The
banks, the state governments, and the people
readily coöperated with the government, and the
New Orleans banks, which had been so well managed that they continued specie payments until
September, 1861, suspended in order to accept
the notes. But long before the end of the second
year the circulation of these exceeded by far the
circulation of United States money in the South in
1860, and they rapidly depreciated. Acts to make
them a legal tender were several times proposed,
but none was passed. Funding acts were passed,
but failed to attain their object. No scheme like
Chase's system of national banks would have been
practicable with the Confederate bonds as a basis,
even if the particularistic public sentiment could
have been overcome to the extent of getting the
necessary law through the Congress. There was
no way to regulate the currency so long as the

notes were issued to pay current expenses. There
was no check on the states, which began to issue
notes before the government. Cities, banks, corporations, business firms, individuals, swelled the
circulation with their promises to pay; counter-
feiters flourished. The currency was redundant,
unregulated, various, fluctuating ; and all the time,
as always when there is too much money, the mass
of the people were clamoring for more and more,
because prices were rising higher and higher.

By the end of 1861, a gold dollar was worth
$1.20 in currency; by the end of 1862, it was
worth $3.00 in currency ; a year later, $20.00;
before the final collapse, $61.00 in paper was paid
for one dollar in gold. Prices in general, with a
few notable exceptions, as of cotton and tobacco,
rose faster and higher than the price of gold.
"Before the war," says a wag in Eggleston's "Recollections," "I went to market with the money in
my pocket, and brought back my purchases in a
basket ; now I take the money in the basket, and
bring the things home in my pocket." Of course,
the waning of the hope of victory would have
depreciated any sort of Confederate obligations,
but victory itself would not have made that un-
soundness sound.

The incitement to speculation was irresistible. The general and correct opinion was that it was better to hold any other sort of property than money. It was because notes, whether they bore interest or not, could be used in ordinary transactions, and for speculation, that they were preferred to bonds. Long-time contracts on a money basis were sure to prove inequitable. Salaries and wages were constantly shrinking. The disposition to economize and be frugal, in which the people had entered upon their time of trial, was followed by a reckless extravagance of the lessening little they had. Business was deranged, industry strangled. Simple-minded patriots laid the blame on the speculators, and there arose once more the growl against the Jews, old as history, heard whenever Gentiles get into trouble over money.

The government saw production curtailed and found the producers less and less minded to sell. It was driven to impressment and arbitrary fixation of prices. In March, 1863, it set up boards of assessment, and from that time continued to force men to sell, at prices below those of the open market, for money sure to depreciate, commodities which they did not wish to sell at all. One result was to discourage industry still further. Another was waste ; for produce, seized wherever found and in whatever condition, often rotted or was stolen or lost before it reached the armies. A third was discontent among the people and dangerous conflicts with states. A Virginia state court granted an injunction to restrain a Confederate official from impressing flour. Governor Brown, of Georgia, protested violently against the law, and the Georgia Supreme Court pronounced it unconstitutional. The feeling against it was particularly strong in North Carolina. Everywhere there was friction in enforcing it.

In general, every strong measure of the government provoked resistance. North Carolina and Georgia were the principal centres of opposition, and their governors, Vance and Brown, the most persistent champions of extreme state rights theories. Robert Toombs, who had been in the Cabinet, and Alexander H. Stephens, the Vice-President, spoke freely on that side. The acts empowering the President to suspend the writ of *habeas corpus*, and the various conscription acts, as they extended the age limits and narrowed the exemptions, with the impressment law, were the measures most stoutly resisted. Brown flatly refused to let a conscription act be enforced in

Georgia. North Carolina courts discharged con-
scripts who had furnished substitutes, and issued
writs of *habeas corpus* in a region where martial
law had been declared. Other measures resisted
were the calling out of the state militia, — a bone
of contention under the old government as far
back as the War of 1812; attempts at regulating
interstate commerce ; the appointing of non-resi-
dents to federal offices in various states; the setting up of government distilleries contrary to state
laws; the taxing of state bonds ; and the effort of
the government to share itself, and to prevent the
states from sharing, in the profits of blockade-
running. Before the end, the opponents of the
government were uniting in a party, strongest in
North Carolina, which avowed its desire for
peace, and asserted the right, though it did not
advocate the policy, of secession from the Confederacy.

For these troubles of the government the Confederate Constitution must be held in part responsible. No government in such straits could have
refrained from arbitrary measures, and the Confederate government could not be arbitrary, it could
not always be trenchant and effective, without
being unconstitutional. Most of the difficulties,

however, would have been encountered if the Constitution had been a word-for-word copy — as it was in most of its paragraphs — of the United States Constitution. The variations from that model were not all of a nature to weaken the central authority. The executive was strengthened. The President's term was lengthened to six years. He could remove the principal officers of the departments, and all officials of the diplomatic service, at his pleasure. He could veto specific items of an appropriation bill; and to this power the Congress, without warrant from the Constitution, added the power to transfer appropriations from one department to another. The power of the legislature was limited by requiring a two-thirds majority in both houses for appropriations not based on department estimates and recommended by the President, by prohibiting extra compensation to public servants, and by prohibiting protection. The sovereignty of the states was expressly affirmed, and slavery guarded from all interference, but public opinion would have made good these provisions if they had been left out. The Supreme Court, though provided for, was never constituted, and no doubt the government was the weaker for want of it; but that, too, was the fault of public opinion.

The assertion that the Confederacy could not have held together in peace is insufficiently sustained if it rests on the differences between the Confederate Constitution and the Constitution of the United States. Stronger and more centralized governments would have been better for the emergency on both sides, but the form which the Confederate government took was the only form it could have taken, and the only form it could have retained in peace. What was in effect a protest against the tendency of the old Union to become a true nation could not have bodied itself forth in a compact and hardy nationality. Unimportant as students know the merits of a written instrument of government to be when they do not accord with material conditions and the character of the civilization to be expressed, the faults of the written instrument are equally unimportant in so far as they are merely departures from a standard which the people cannot or will not live up to.

To follow the inner workings of the Confederacy, as we are now enabled to do, will supply political scientists and public men with striking instances of the effects of defying economic laws and disobeying the rules of sound finance. It will reveal more clearly than ever the industrial backwardness of the South, and emphasize that as the most serious of its disadvantages in the struggle. It will credit President Davis and his advisers, and many other civil servants of the Confederacy, with the utmost zeal and much intelligence, but none of them with great practical and constructive statesmanship. It will show the Congress at Richmond to have been a weak and undistinguished legislature. It will confirm completely our feeling that the armies of the South were finer far than anything they defended, — that the wonderful gray shell was of greater worth than all it held. To our main inquiry, the answer is that the failure of the Southerners to win their independence, clearly as it should have been foreseen, *was*, in quite definite ways, immediately attributable to faults and errors.

But to dwell on these faults and errors, to make our study wholly common-sense and scientific, may easily mislead us. It may lead us to neglect the strength, while we search out the weakness, of the South. It may lead us away from the moving spectacle of a resolute and devoted people, hard beset by a stronger adversary, and struggling with the defects of its own civilization, which will survive when the economic and political lessons to be got from the rise and fall of the Confederacy shall have lost their value.

That was what Mr. Henley's sailor saw from the Charleston wharf.

" In and out among the cotton,
    Mud, and chains, and stores, and anchors,
    Tramped a crew of battered scare-crows,
    Poor old Dixie's bottom dollars.

" Some had shoes, but all had bayonets,
    Them that wasn't bald was beardless,
    And the drum was rolling *Dixie*,
    And they stepped to it like men, sir.

" Rags and tatters, belts and bayonets,
    On they swung, the drum a-rolling,
    Mum and sour.   It looked like fighting,
    And they meant it too, by thunder ! "

# IV.  THE KU KLUX MOVEMENT

# IV

## THE KU KLUX MOVEMENT

WHOEVER can remember Mr. Edwin Booth in
the character of Richelieu will doubtless recall
his expression of the sudden change which
comes over the melodramatic cardinal toward
the end of the scene in which his house is
invaded by the conspirators. While he is ignorant of his danger, his helplessness in the grasp
of his swarming enemies, Richelieu is all majesty, all tragedy. But when he learns that
every avenue of escape is barred, that even
Huguet is false, that no open force will avail
him, his towering mood gives place, not indeed
to any cringing fear, but to subtlety and swift
contriving. His eyes no longer blaze, but
twinkle; his finger is at his chin; there is a
semblance of a grin about his lips.

"All? Then the lion's skin's too short to-night,—
Now for the fox's."

The deathbed stratagem follows. The enemy,
too powerful to be resisted, is outwitted and
befooled.

About the year 1870, if a Southern negro inquired of his former master about " dem Ku Kluxes," the response he got was awe-inspiring. If a child of the household made the same inquiry of his elders, his question was put away with an unsatisfying answer and a look like Mr. Booth's in the play. Had the great cardinal lived south of Mason and Dixon's line in the late sixties and early seventies, I fancy he would have found the Ku Klux Klan an instrument altogether to his liking.

The Southern child who, not content with the grin and the evasive answer of his father or his elder brother, sought further enlightenment from his fast friends of the kitchen and the quarters, heard such stories of the mysterious, sheeted brotherhood as eclipsed in his young fancy even the entrancing rivalry of Brer Fox and Brer Rabbit, and made the journey back to the "big house" at bedtime a terrifying experience. Uncle Lewis would tell of a shrouded horseman who rode silently up to his door at midnight, begged a drink of water, and tossed off a whole bucketful at a draught. Uncle Lewis was sure he could hear the water sizzling as it flowed down that monstrous gullet, and readily accepted the stranger's explanation that it was the first

drop he had tasted since he was killed at Shi-
loh. Aunt Lou, coming home from a visit to
a neighboring auntie who was ill, and cross-
ing a lonesome stretch near the graveyard, had
distinctly seen a group of horsemen, motionless
by the roadside, each with his head in his hand.
Alec, a young mulatto who had once displayed
much interest in politics, had been stopped on
his way from a meeting of his "s'iety" by
a masked horseman, at least eight feet tall, who
insisted on shaking hands; and when Alec grasped
the hand outstretched to him, it was the hand
of a skeleton. Darkies who, unlike Uncle Lewis
and Aunt Lou and Alec, had turned against
their own white people and taken up with the
carpet-baggers had been more roughly handled.

Somehow, in one such Southern boy's memory, there is always a dim association of these
Ku Klux stories with other stories of the older
negroes about "patterrollers." Through them
all there jingles the refrain : —

> "Run, nigger, run !
> De patterrollers ketch you ! "

When that boy went to college and joined a
society that had initiations, the mystery and
horror of the Ku Klux stories waned; but it

was not until he read an account of the patrol
system of slavery times that he saw the connection between Ku Klux and "patterrollers."

An organization which could so mystify all
but the grown-up white men of a Southern
household certainly lost none of its mystery in the
confused accounts that filled the newspapers of
that day, and citizens of the Northern states,
already tired of the everlasting Southern question,
could not be expected to understand it. Congress, when it undertook to enlighten them, swelled
its records with much impassioned oratory, and
through its committees of investigation put into
print first one and then thirteen bulky volumes of
reports and testimony, from which he who lives
long enough to read it all may learn much that is
true but not particularly important, much that
is important if true, and somewhat that is both
true and important. From the mass of it the
Republican majority got matter sufficient to sustain one set of conclusions, leaving unused enough
to sustain quite as strongly the entirely different
conclusions at which the minority arrived. There
remained much upon which the novelists, whether
humorously or sensationally inclined, have drawn
and may continue to draw. Dr. Conan Doyle,

seeking to "paint a horror skilfully," found the Klan a good nerve-racker, though it is to be hoped he did not attempt to digest the reports. Voluminous as they are, they need to be supplemented with material of a different sort, — with such memories as the child of reconstruction times can summon up, with such written memoranda and cautious talk as can be won from Southerners of an older generation, with such insight as one can get into Southern character and habits of thought and life, — before one can begin to understand what the Klan was, or how it came into existence, or what its part was in that great confusion officially styled the Reconstruction of the Southern states.

We may, I think, forbear argument and take it for granted that the Ku Klux movement was an outcome of the conditions that prevailed in the Southern states after the war. It was too widespread, too spontaneous, too clearly a popular movement, to be attributed to any one man or to any conspiracy of a few men. Had it existed only in one corner of the South, or drawn its membership from a small and sharply defined class, some such explanation might serve. But we know enough of its extent, its composition, and the various forms it took, to feel sure that it was neither an accident nor a mere scheme. It was no man's contrivance, but an historical development. As such, it must be studied against its proper background of a disordered society and a bewildered people.

It will be necessary here to emphasize only one feature of the general misgovernment: namely, that the evil was by no means confined to the state governments, where the bolder adventurers and the more stupendous blunderers were at work. The itching and galling of the yoke was worst in the lesser communities, where government touches the lives of individual men and women most intimately. The mismanagement — to use the mildest word — of the finances of the states can be shown in figures with reasonable clearness. The oppression of counties and towns and school districts is less easily exhibited, though it was in this way the heaviest burdens of taxation were imposed. The total increase in the indebtedness of the smaller political units under carpet-bag rule was, as a matter of fact, even greater than in the case of the state governments; and the wrong was done in plainer view of the taxpayer, by acts more openly and vulgarly tyrannical. So far as the taxpayer's feelings were concerned, piling up state debts had the effect which the mismanagement of a bank has on the stockholders. The piling up of county and town and school taxes was like thrusting hands visibly and forcibly into his pockets. It is doubtful, however, if even the injury to his fortunes had so much to do with his state of mind as the countless humiliations and irritations which the rule of the freedman and the stranger brought upon him.

If the white man of the class long dominant in the South was permitted to vote at all, he might have literally to pass under bayonets to reach the polls. He saw freedmen organized in militia companies, expensively armed and gayly caparisoned ; if he offered his own military services, they were sure to be rejected. He saw his former slaves repeating at elections, but he learned that he had no right of challenge, and that there was no penalty fixed by law for the crime. In the local courts of justice, he saw his friends brought by an odious system of informers before judges who were not merely incompetent or unfair, like many of those who sat in the higher courts, but often grotesquely ignorant as well, and who intrusted the execution of their instruments to officials who in many cases could not write an intelligible return. In the schools which he was so heavily taxed to support, he saw the children of his slaves getting book-learning, which he himself thought it unwise to give them, from strangers who would be sure to train them into discontent with the only lot he thought them fit for and the only sort of work which, in the world he knew, they ever had a chance to do. He saw the Freedmen's Bureau deliberately trying to substitute its alien machinery for that patriarchal relation between white employers and black workmen which had seemed to him right and inevitable. He saw the Loyal League urging freedmen to take up those citizenly powers and duties which, when he gave up his sword, he had never understood emancipation to imply for them. In every boisterous shout of a drunken negro before his gate, in every insolent glance from a group of idle negroes on the streets of the county seat, in the reports of fisticuffs with little darkies which his children brought home from school, in the noises of the night and the glare of occasional conflagrations, he saw the hand or heard the harshly accented voice of the stranger in the land.

It seems astounding, nowadays, that the con-

gressional leaders in reconstruction did not fore-
see that men of their own stock, so beset, would
resist, and would find some means to make
their resistance effective. When they did make
up their minds to resist, — not collectively, or
through any representative body, but singly and
by neighborhoods, — they found an instrument
ready to their hands.

When the Civil War ended, the little town of
Pulaski, Tennessee, welcomed home a band of
young men who, though they were veterans
of hard-fought fields, were for the most part no
older than the mass of college students. In the
general poverty, the exhaustion, the loss of heart,
naturally prevalent throughout the beaten South,
young men had more leisure than was good for
them. A Southern country town, even in the
halcyon days before the war, was not a particularly lively place; and Pulaski in 1866 was doubtless rather tame to fellows who had seen Pickett's
charge at Gettysburg or galloped over the country
with Morgan and Wheeler. A group of them,
gathered in a law office one evening in May,
1866, were discussing ways and means of having
a livelier time. Some one suggested a club or
society. An organization with no very definite

aims was effected, and at a second meeting, a week later, names were proposed and discussed. Some one pronounced the Greek word " Kuklos," meaning a circle. From "Kuklos" to "Ku Klux" was an easy transition, — whoever consults a glossary of college boys' slang will not find it strange, — and " Klan " followed " Ku Klux " as naturally as "Dumpty" follows "Humpty." That the name meant nothing whatever was a recommendation ; and one can fancy what sort of badinage would have greeted a suggestion that in six years a committee of Congress would devote thirteen volumes to the history of the " movement " that began in a Pulaski law office and migrated later to a deserted and half-ruined house in the outskirts of the village.

In the beginning, it was, in fact, no "movement" at all. It was a scheme for having fun, more like a college secret society than anything else. Its members were not "lewd fellows of the baser sort," but young men of standing in the community, who would also have been men of wealth if there had been no war. The main source of amusement was at first the initiation of new members, but later the puzzling of outsiders. The only important clause in the oath of membership was a promise of absolute secrecy. The disguise was a white mask, a tall cardboard hat, a gown or robe that covered the whole person, and also, when the Klan went mounted, a cover for the horses' bodies and some sort of muffling for their feet. The chief officers were a Grand Cyclops, or president; a Grand Magi, or vice-president; a Grand Turk, or marshal; a Grand Exchequer, or treasurer; and two Lictors. While the club adhered to its original aim and character, only men of known good morals were admitted. Born of the same impulse and conditions that had led to the "snipe hunt" and other hazing devices of Southern country towns, it was probably as harmless and as unimportant a piece of fooling as any to be found inside or outside of colleges.

The Klan was eminently successful. It got all the notoriety it wished, and very soon the youth of neighboring communities began to organize "dens" of their own. The mysterious features of the Klan were most impressive, and it spread most rapidly, in rural neighborhoods. Probably it would have become a permanent secret society, not unlike the better known of the unserious secret orders which are so common throughout the South to-day, but for the state of Southern politics and the progress of Reconstruction. These things, however, soon gave a tremendous importance to the Klan's inevitable discovery that mystery and fear have over the African mind twice the power they have over the mind of a white man. It was not the first instance in history of a movement which began in mere purposeless fooling ending in the most serious way. By the time Congress had thrown aside the gentle and kindly plan of reconstruction which Lincoln conceived and Johnson could not carry out, the Ku Klux had taught the white men of Tennessee and neighboring states the power of mystery over the credulous race which Congress was bent on intrusting with the most difficult tasks of citizenship. When Southern society, turned upside down, groped about for some means of righting itself, it grasped the Pulaski idea.

As it happened, Tennessee, the original home of the Klan, was the very state in which reconstruction began earliest; and though the course of events there was somewhat different from the experience of the Cotton states, Tennessee was also the first state to find its social and governmental systems

upside down. It was notable for its large Unionist population. The Unionists were strongest in
the mountainous eastern half of the state, while
the western half, dominant before the war, was
strongly secessionist. The first step in Reconstruction was to put the east Tennesseeans into
power; and the leader of the east Tennessee
Unionists was "Parson" Brownlow. Apart from
his Unionism, Brownlow is generally conceded
to have been an extremely unfit man for great
public responsibilities, and when he became governor the secessionists had to endure much the
same sort of misgovernment which in other
states was attributable to carpet-bag officials.
By the time it was a year old, the Klan had
gradually developed into a society of regula-
tors, using its peculiar devices and its acciden-
tally discovered power chiefly to repress the
lawlessness into which white men of Brownlow's
following were sometimes led by their long-
nourished grudge against their former rulers,
and into which freedmen fell so inevitably that
no fair-minded historian can mete out to them
a hard measure of censure for it. In the Union
League the Klan found its natural enemy; and
it is quite probably true that, during the early

period of their rivalry for control, more inexcusable violence proceeded from the League than from the Klan.

However, a survivor and historian of the Klan does not deny that even thus early the abuses inseparable from secrecy existed in the order. To suppress them, and to adapt the order to its new and serious work, a convention was held at Nashville early in 1867. The Klan, up to that time bound together only by a general deference to the Grand Cyclops of the Pulaski "Den," was organized into the "Invisible Empire of the South," ruled by a Grand Wizard of the whole Empire, a Grand Dragon of each Realm, or state, a Grand Titan of each Dominion (Province), or county, a Grand Cyclops of each Den, and staff officers with names equally terrifying. The objects of the Klan, now that it had serious objects, were defined. They were, to protect the people from indignities and wrongs; to succor the suffering, particularly the families of dead Confederate soldiers; to defend "the Constitution of the United States, and all laws passed in conformity thereto," and of the states also; and to aid in executing all constitutional laws, and protect the people from

unlawful seizures and from trial otherwise than
by jury. Acts of the Brownlow legislature re-
viving the alien and sedition laws were particularly aimed at.

From this time, the Klan put itself more
clearly in evidence, generally adhering to its
original devices of mystery and silence, but too
often yielding to the temptation to add to these
violence. On the night of July 4, by well-
heralded parades, it exhibited itself throughout
Tennessee, and perhaps in other states, more
impressively than ever before. At Pulaski, some
four hundred disguised horsemen marched and
countermarched silently through the streets
before thousands of spectators, and not a single
disguise was penetrated. The effect of mystery
even on intelligent minds was well illustrated in
the estimate, made by "reputable citizens," that
the number was not less than three thousand.
Members who lived in the town averted suspicion from themselves by appearing undisguised
among the spectators. A gentleman who prided
himself on knowing every horse in the county
attempted to identify one by lifting its robe,
only to discover that the animal and the saddle
were his own!

The remaining facts in the history of the
Ku Klux proper need not be told at length.
The effectiveness of the order was shown wherever, by its original methods, it exerted itself to
quiet disturbed communities.  Wherever freedmen
grew unruly, disguised horsemen appeared by
night, and thereafter the darkies of the neighborhood inclined to stay under cover after day-
light failed.  But the order had grown too large,
it was too widespread, the central authority was
too remote from the local " dens," and the general scheme was too easily grasped and copied.
It was too hard to keep out such men as
would incline to use violence, or to cover
with the mantle of secrecy enterprises of a
doubtful or even criminal cast.  In Tennessee,
the Brownlow government was bitterly hostile,
and in September, 1868, the legislature passed a
statute, aimed entirely at the Ku Klux, which
went beyond the later congressional statutes in
the penalties it prescribed for every act that
could possibly imply complicity in the " conspiracy," and in the extraordinary powers it con-
ferred upon officers and all others who should
aid in detecting or arresting Ku Klux.  The
members of the order were practically outlawed,

and felt themselves justified in resorting to measures of self-defence which the central officers could not approve. In February, 1869, Governor Brownlow proclaimed martial law in several Tennessee counties. His term of office expired the next day. The growing evils within the order, as well as the dangers which threatened it, doubtless made the wiser heads of the Klan readier to conclude that with the repeal of the alien and sedition laws, and Brownlow's departure for the United States Senate, its work in Tennessee was done. So, a few weeks later, by an order of the Grand Wizard, the Klan was formally disbanded, not only in Tennessee, but everywhere. It is generally understood that the Grand Wizard who issued that order was no less a person than Nathan Bedford Forrest. How many dens ever received the order, and how many of those that received it also obeyed it, will never be known, any more than it will be known how many dens there were, or how many members. However, the early spring of 1869 may be taken as the date when the Ku Klux Klan, which gave its name and its idea to the secret movement which began the undoing of reconstruction, ceased to exist as an organized body.

But the history of the original Ku Klux Klan is only a part — and perhaps not the most important part — of the movement which in the North was called the Ku Klux conspiracy, and which in the South is to this day regarded, with a truer sense of its historical importance, whatever one may think of its moral character, as comparable to that secret movement by which, under the very noses of French garrisons, Stein and Scharnhorst organized the great German struggle for liberty. Of the disguised bands which appeared and disappeared throughout the South so long as the carpet-baggers controlled the state governments, it is probable that not one-half were veritable Ku Klux. Some were members of other orders, founded in imitation of the Ku Klux, and using similar methods. Others were probably neighborhood affairs only. Yet others were simply bands of ruffians who operated in the night-time and availed themselves of Ku Klux methods to attain personal ends which, whether criminal or not, were not approved by the leaders in the Ku Klux and other similar organizations. How large a proportion of the

violence and crime attributed to the Ku Klux
should rightly be attributed to these lawless bands,
it is, of course, impossible to say. It seems that
a number of those taken in disguise proved to
be men of such antecedents, so clearly identified
with the radical party, that they could not possibly have been members of the Ku Klux, the
Knights of the White Camellia, or any other of
the orders whose *raison d'être* was the revolt
against radical rule. But it is equally beyond
question that the orders themselves were responsible for many indefensible proceedings.

The order of the Knights of the White Camellia
was probably the largest and most important of
them all — larger even than the true Ku Klux
Klan. It was founded at New Orleans late in
1867 or early in 1868 and spread rapidly over
the states to the east and west, from Texas to
the Carolinas. A constitution adopted in June,
1868, provided for an elaborate organization by
states, counties, and smaller communities, the
affairs of the whole order to be committed to a
supreme council at New Orleans. The recollec-
tion of members, however, is to the effect that
very little authority was really exercised by the
supreme council or even by the state councils,

that the county organizations were reasonably
well maintained, but that in most respects each
circle acted independently.  The constitution and
the oath and ceremonial of initiation commit the
order to a very clear and decided stand on
the chief question of the day.  Only white men
eighteen years of age or older were admitted,
and the initiate promised not merely to be secret
and obedient, but "to maintain and defend the
social and political superiority of the white race on
this continent."  The charge or lecture to the
initiate set forth historical evidences of the superiority of the white race, made an argument for
white supremacy, and painted the horrors of
miscegenation.  It enjoined fairness to negroes,
and the concession to them of "the fullest
measure of those rights which we recognize as
theirs."  The association, so the charge explained,
was not a political party, and had no connection
with any.  The constitution, moreover, restrained
the order from nominating or supporting candidates for office.

The "Pale Faces," the "Constitutional Union
Guards," the "White Brotherhood," were other
names borne by bands of men who did Ku Klux
work.  The majority of the congressional com-

mittee somehow got the notion that these were
the real names, at different periods, of the one
order which pervaded the entire South, and that
"Ku Klux" was a name foisted on the public
to the end that a member, when put upon the
witness stand in a law court, might deny all
knowledge of the organization. But the evidence
of the existence of the true Ku Klux Klan, of
its priority to all similar organizations of any
importance, and of the existence of other orders
with different names, is now too strong to permit
of any doubt. The comparative strength of the
various associations; the connection, if any there
was, between them; the character of their membership; the differences in their aims and methods;
— on these things it is not probable that any clear
light will ever be thrown. Surviving members
are themselves somewhat hazy on such questions.
And indeed it is not of the first importance that
they should be answered; for we have enough
to show how the Ku Klux idea worked itself out,
and with what results.

The working of the plan is exhibited, more
authoritatively than I could portray it, in the
memoranda of a gentle and kindly man, albeit
a resolute wearer of a Confederate button, who,

thirty years ago, was the absolute chief of the Knights of the White Camellia in a certain county in the heart of the Black Belt. Speaking of the county organization merely, he says : —

"The authority of the commander (this office I held) was *absolute*. All were sworn to obey his orders. There was an inner circle in each circle, to which was committed any particular work : its movements were not known to other members of the order. This was necessary, because, in our neighborhood, almost every Southern man was a member. At meetings of the full circle there was but little consideration as to work. The topic generally was law and order, and the necessity for organization. In fact, almost every meeting might have been public, so far as the discussions were concerned.

"For the methods employed : in some cases they were severe, even extreme, but I believe they were necessary, although there was much wrong done when commanders were not the right men. There was too good an opportunity for individuals to take vengeance for personal grievances. A man, black or white, found dead in the road would furnish undisputed evidence that the Ku Klux Klan had been abroad. The officers of the law, even judges, were members; a jury could not be drawn without a majority of our men. In this county, no act of violence was committed by our circle. We operated on the terror inspired by the knowledge that we were organized. The carpet-baggers lived in constant dread of a visit, and were in great measure controlled through their fears. At one time, if one of our people threatened or abused a carpet-bagger, his house or stable would be fired that night.[1] . . . This occurred so often that it was impossible to separate the two events. Word was accordingly sent to a prominent carpet-bagger that if the thing happened again we would take him out at midday and hang him. There were no more fires.

"The negroes had meetings at some point every night, in obedience to the orders of the carpet-baggers, who kept them organized in this way. So long as their meetings were orderly, we did not interfere; but when I got information that they were becoming disorderly and offensive, I ordered out a body of horsemen, who divided into squads

[1] Here he refers to the oiling and firing of the stables of that particular Southern household in which the boyish inquiries I have referred to made a beginning of the investigations on which this paper is based.

and stationed themselves where the negroes would pass on their way home. They were permitted to dress themselves in any fashion their fancies might dictate, but their orders were positive not to utter a word or molest a negro in any manner. I rarely had to send twice to the same neighborhood. Occasionally a large body was sent out to ride about all night, with the same instructions as to silence. While the law against illegal voting had no penalty for the offence (no doubt an intentional omission) negroes often voted more than once at the same election. They assembled in such crowds at the polls that one had almost to fight one's way to deposit a ballot. A body of our men was detailed on election day to go early and take possession, with the usual order for silence. Few negroes voted that day; none twice. No violence.

"We put up with carpet-bag rule as long as we could stand it. Then a messenger was sent to each of them — they were filling all the county offices — to tell them we had decided they must leave. This was all that was needed. They had been expecting it, they said, and they left without making any resistance. Owing to some local circumstances, the circle at —— was disbanded about the time of President Grant's proclamation, but we were not influenced by it in any degree. I think there were few cases of the disbandment of circles. The necessity for their existence expired with the exodus of the carpet-baggers."

That was the *modus operandi*, under a cautious and intelligent commander, in a neighborhood largely inhabited by men of birth and education. As it happens, the recollections of the commander are corroborated by one of the young men who obeyed his orders, now attorney-general of the state, who adds that the proportion of "tomfoolery" to violence was about 1000 to 1. But even this straightforward recital of the successful performance of an apparently commendable work must make plain to any thoughtful reader the danger inseparable from the power of such an organization. In communities less intelligent, or where no such fit leader was chosen, the story was far different.

That violence was often used cannot be denied. Negroes were often whipped, and so were carpet-baggers. The incidents related in such stories as Tourgée's "A Fool's Errand" all have their counterparts in the testimony before congressional committees and courts of law. In some cases, after repeated warnings, men were dragged from their beds and slain by persons in disguise, and the courts were unable to find or to convict the murderers. Survivors of the orders affirm that such work was done in most cases by persons not connected with them or acting under their authority. It is impossible to prove or disprove their statements. When such outrages were committed, not on worthless adventurers, who had no station in the Northern communities from which they came, but on cultivated persons who had gone South from genuinely philanthropic motives, — no matter how unwisely or tactlessly they went about their work, — the natural effect was to horrify and enrage the North.

The white teachers in the negro schools were probably the class which suffered most innocently, not ordinarily from violence, but from the countless other ways in which Southern society made them aware that they were unwelcome and that their mission was disapproved. They themselves, in too many instances, disregarded the boundary lines between different social classes, as rigid and cruel in democracies as anywhere else. Associating constantly with freedmen, they could not reasonably expect any kindly recognition from men and women who, under other conditions, might have been their friends. They too often not merely disregarded, but even criticised and attacked, those usages and traditions which gave to Southern life a charm and distinction not elsewhere found in America. A wiser and more candid study of the conditions under which their work must be done, an avoidance of all hostility to whatever they might leave alone without sacrifice of principle, would perhaps have tempered the bitterness of Southern resentment at their presence. We may also admit that the sort of education they at first offered the freedmen was useless, or worse than useless, — that theirs *was* a fool's errand. But they should never have been confounded with the creatures who came, not to help the negro, but to use him. The worst work the Ku Klux ever did was its opposition to negro schools, and the occasional expulsion or even violent handling of teachers. There were adventurers in the schoolhouses, and probably there were honest men in the legislatures, the courts, the executive offices; but as a class the teachers were far better than the others. The failure to discriminate in their favor doubtless did more than anything else to confirm the minds of honest and well-meaning people of the North in the belief that it was the baser elements of Southern society, and not its intelligent and responsible men, who had set to work to overthrow the carpet-bag régime.

The Ku Klux movement was not entirely underground. Sheeted horsemen riding about in the night-time were not its only forces. Secrecy and silence were indeed its main devices, but others were employed. The life of the carpet-bagger was made wretched otherwise than by dragging him from his bed and flogging him. The scorn in which he was held was made plain to him by averted faces or contemptuous glances on the street, by the obstacles he encountered in business, by the empty pews in his neighborhood when he went to church. If his children went to school, they were not asked to join in the play of other children, and must perforce fall back upon the companionship of little darkies. He himself, if he took the Southern view of "difficulties," and held himself ready to answer an insult with a blow, was sure to be accommodated whenever he felt belligerent. Probably not one in ten of his neighbors had given up the creed of the duello, though its ceremonial was not often observed. As for the "scalawag," — the Southerner who went over to the radicals, —

there was reserved for him a deeper hatred, a loftier contempt, than even the carpet-bagger got for his portion. No alien enemy, however despicable, is ever so loathed as a renegade.

But the Invisible Empire, however its sway was exercised, was everywhere a real empire. Wisely and humanely, or roughly and cruelly and criminally, the work was done. The state governments, under radical control, made little headway with their freedmen's militia against the silent representatives of the white man's will to rule. After 1870, even the blindest of the Reconstruction leaders in Congress were made to see that they had built their house upon the sands. During the winter of 1870-71, Southern outrages were the subject of congressional debates and presidential messages. In March, a Senate committee presented majority and minority reports on the result of its investigations in North Carolina. The majority found that there was a criminal conspiracy, of a distinctly political nature, against the laws and against colored citizens. The minority found that the misgovernment and the unscrupulous exploiting of the Southern states by radical leaders had provoked a natural resistance and led to disorder and violence. In April, the first Ku Klux bill, "to enforce the Fourteenth Amendment," was passed; the President was empowered to use the troops, and even to suspend the writ of *habeas corpus*. The second Ku Klux bill, "to enforce the right of citizens of the United States to vote," was passed in May. In October, the President issued his proclamation. Troops were freely employed wherever there was an opportunity to use them, and the writ was suspended in nine counties of South Carolina. Hundreds of men were brought to trial before United States courts under the two laws, and a number were convicted; but the leading men in the great orders were never reached. Northern writers have expressed the opinion that by the beginning of 1872 the "conspiracy" was overthrown. Nevertheless, the joint committee proceeded with its labors, and in February presented its great report on The Condition of Affairs in the Late Insurrectionary States. Majority and minority differed, as before; but the volume of reports and the twelve volumes of testimony enabled the one side to prove more conclusively that crimes had been committed for political ends, and the other to set forth with more convincing fulness the true nature of carpet-bag rule. In May, a bill extending the President's extraordinary powers over to the next session of Congress passed the Senate, but was lost in the House. How much the action of Congress and the President had to do with the disappearance of the Ku Klux, it is impossible to say. But·after 1872 the Ku Klux did, for the most part, disappear ; and so, in one state after another, did the carpet-bagger and the scalawag. The fox's skin had served its turn before it was cast aside.

Such, in brief outline, was the Ku Klux conspiracy according to the Northern view, the revolt against tyranny according to the Southern view, which was the beginning of the end of Reconstruction. It was the unexpected outcome of a situation unexampled, and not even closely paralleled, in history. To many minds, it seemed to nullify the war, the Emancipation Proclamation, and the constitutional amendments which were meant to seal forever the victory of the North over the South, and of liberty over slavery. To minds just as honest, it seemed to reassert the great principles of the American Revolution. The majority of the congressional committee conducted their investigation after the manner of prosecuting attorneys dealing with ordinary criminals. The minority felt themselves bound to consider whether " an indictment against a whole people" would lie. To the majority, "Ku Klux" meant simply outlaws; the minority thought that the first Ku Klux in history were the disguised men who, against the law, threw the tea overboard in Boston Harbor.

The two views of the movement, like the movement itself, and all that led up to it, are part and parcel of that division which was marked by Mason and Dixon's line. It was a division of institutions; it was a division of interests; it was, and is still, a division of character and habits of thought. Northern men had one idea of the strife, and Southern men an entirely different idea. The Southerners did not and could not regard themselves as rebels forced to be loyal. They knew they were beaten, and they gave up the fight; but they could not see how they were bound to coöperate in any further plans of their conquerors. President Lincoln had made it plain that if the Union arms prevailed slavery must go, and the Southerners, in their state conventions of 1865, formally abolished it. Secession had been tried, and had failed as a policy; they declared that they would not try it again. Left for a moment to themselves, they set to work on an arrangement that would enable them to use under freedom the same sort of labor they had used under slavery, and made a place in the new order for the blacks, whom they could not reduce to slavery again, but whom they felt to be unfit for citizenship. Then Congress interfered and undid their work, and they stood passive until they could see what the congressional scheme would be like. They found it bad, oppressive, unwise, impossible. They bore it awhile in silence. Then in silence they made up their minds to resist. What form could their resistance take? It must be revolutionary, for they had formally renounced the right of secession. It could not be open war, for they were powerless to fight. So they made a secret revolution. Their rebellion could not raise its head, so it went underground.

If one asks of the movement, "Was it necessary?" this much, at least, may be answered: that no other plan of resistance would have served so well. If one asks, "Was it successful?" the answer is plain. No open revolt ever succeeded more completely. If one asks, "Was it justifiable?" the "yes" or "no" is harder to say. There must be much defining of terms, much patient separating of the accidental from the essential, much inquiry into motives. Describe the movement broadly as a secret movement, operating by terror and violence to nullify laws, and one readily condemns it. Paint all the conditions, enter into the minds and hearts of the men who lived under them, look at them through their eyes, suffer with their angry pain, and one revolts as their pride revolted. Weigh the broad rule, which is less a "light to guide" than a "rod to check," against the human impulse, and the balance trembles. One is ready to declare, not, perhaps, that the end justified the means, but that never before was an end so clearly worth fighting for made so clearly unattainable by any good means.

Nor does our hindsight much avail us. The end attained was mainly good. Southern society was righted. But the method of it survives in too many habits of the Southern mind, in too many shortcomings of Southern civilization, in too many characteristics of Southern life. The Southern whites, solidified in resistance to carpet-bag rule, have kept their solidarity unimpaired by any healthful division on public questions. Having learned a lesson, they cannot forget it. Having seen forms of law used to cloak oppression, and liberty invoked to countenance a tyranny, they learned to set men above political principles, and good government above freedom of thought. For thirty years they have continued to set one question above all others, and thus debarred themselves from full participation in the political life of the country. As they rule by fear, so by fear are they ruled. It is they themselves who are now befooled, and robbed of the nobler part of their own political birthright. They outdid their conquerors, yet they are not free.

# V. A NEW HERO OF AN OLD TYPE

# V

# A NEW HERO OF AN OLD TYPE

In nothing was the national sense of the emergency in which we found ourselves in consequence of the war with Spain more clearly shown than in the popular feeling toward the men who distinguished themselves in the fighting. The man who could fight for us was the man of the hour. But yesterday, the politician had overshadowed him; even the man of letters had held a higher place in our regard. The purveyor of amusement knew him, indeed, as a picturesque figure on the stage; but how many of us, as we turned from the burial of the great captains of the Civil War, gave a serious thought to the men at the head of our diminutive army? How many of us even knew who commanded the Asiatic squadron until the newspapers set us listening for the cannonade on the other side of the world? As to the young hero, many of us, no doubt, were fondly hoping that as the world grew gentler some other figure might take his place in our hearts. He seemed to belong to the past, to history and drama and poetry, until suddenly we found ourselves in need of him. As suddenly, and with every dramatical accompaniment, through the battle smoke and dim light of the dawn at Santiago, he appeared. Again he took his ancient place in our hearts, as in the van of our enterprise. The sudden need of him was distressing, but who of all our millions was not brighter eyed when he came ?

The fitness of American soldiers and sailors to do our fighting became an object of serious inquiry only when it was too late to make any radical changes in our military and naval methods before the trial. The West-Pointer at his dreary post on the frontier, the naval officer testing his projectiles, were less interesting than the college athlete on the foot-ball field or in the racing shell. We took little thought of the men who must now represent us before England, which expected so much of us, and before Europe, which apparently expected so little. To show that there was courage and skill at the head of our armaments was the part of Admiral Dewey. To prove that heroism of the highest military type abounded in the breasts of the generation on which the fighting work of the war must fall, and likewise the later work, which the war would entail, was the opportunity of eight men at Santiago. To associate a name altogether new to larger history with the shining names of those who have from time to time illustrated the capacity of his race for masterful handling of danger was the supreme privilege of a youth whose deserts it is well for us to know, since otherwise we might not feel sure of the justice of fame's award, and whose character and training are still very important subjects of reflection, since he stands so conspicuously for his fellows in our service.

When the American fleet first advanced toward the Cuban shores, the human element in its iron might was typified for me by a single boyish figure outlined against a background utterly unsuggestive of the sea, but a figure none the less suggestive of all that is essential in the man behind the gun. The night before we heard the news of the *Merrimac* exploit, a name was often on my lips, joined, in comfortable talk, with the prediction that only failure of opportunity could keep it obscure. The next day, the name was famous, and the boyish figure, enlarged to Homeric manhood, erect and masterful on the perilous bridge of the *Merrimac*, was for the moment quite the most notable figure in the world.

The emergency and the mood of the nation made that earlier background of young Hobson's figure peculiarly important ; for it was a background of cotton fields and newly liberated slaves. It is surely a hopeful augury that our first young hero came to us from the one region from which we had, apparently, better reason to expect imperfect devotion to the Republic than from any other ; a region from which the more ignorant of our adversaries actually expected aid and comfort.

Thirty years ago, the South was not a source of confidence to the champions of American democracy. Americans were in worse state there than they have been anywhere else or at any other time. Defeated in a long war, impoverished, and given over to a hard rule, the men who there represented the English race were as near despair as Englishmen have ever been since the Armada. A child's face is apt to take on the expression of the faces around it, and the faces of men and women in Alabama in the early seventies were not happy faces, as a rule. It was patience that shone clearest on the women's brows. The biographer of the late Justice Lamar makes a very striking picture of the man one might have seen in those

days in the little town of Oxford, Mississippi, lean-
ing stolidly over the ruinous fence in front of his
house, heavy-browed, coatless, the great mass of
his hair and beard neglected and unkempt, ac-
knowledging with a surly nod the greetings of his
acquaintance. A bright-eyed young editor in
Atlanta, naturally of a joyous temper, used to sit
for hours gazing abstractedly out of the window
of his cheerless office; in another country, he
might very well have fallen under suspicion of
meditating sedition.

The boy whom I first knew among the Alabama
cotton fields was grave-faced. His manner was
stiff and formal; his conversation, almost comi-
cally stilted. One might have thought him heavy-
natured if it had not been for his eyes. In
them there was a smouldering fierceness which
I did not understand, for his bearing was modest
to gentleness, and his voice had all the drawl-
ing sweetness of the leisurely civilization out of
which he came. Sometimes, however, in base-
ball and other sports, it had a tone of authority
which provoked less resistance than an attitude
of superiority is apt to provoke among people in
whom association with a subject race has bred an
imperious temper. For the rest, he stood out

from his fellows chiefly by reason of the steadfastness with which he kept in mind the possibility of an honorable career and the fearlessness with which he addressed himself to the more serious concerns of boyhood. That attitude toward life was somewhat remarkable, for the shadow of defeat, the reality of suffering, made doggedness commoner than ambition.

Many of the older men failed altogether to take heart for new careers. In men of the coarser sort, Reconstruction had bred more bitterness of sectional feeling than the war itself had produced. The weaker sort simply went to the wall. But it is clear now that neither the coarse nor the weak were the representative men of the South, even under conditions so unfamiliar to the race as prevailed there in Reconstruction times. Lamar's stony silence, unbroken since his voice was heard in the Mississippi secession convention, was broken at last in fervent eulogy of the dead Sumner, the champion of human freedom. The Atlanta editor won a sudden and unexampled eminence as the orator of a new patriotism in the reconstructed South. The grave-faced boy, deliberately consecrated to the flag against which his father and his kindred had fought in many battles, gave the best

possible proof that it is the flag of a united people;
he put into a glorious deed, and not into mere
eloquent words, the protestations of Lamar and
Grady. For Americans, in whom there is no
finer quality than ready trust, their words were
perhaps sufficient; but his deed was for the
world.

This especial significance of the deed is enough
to make it memorable; it exhibited a patriotism
which was itself, in some degree, an achievement,
and Americans everywhere welcomed it for that
reason. But the deed in its own character was
representative in a far broader sense than this.
It is a fit deed to stand for us whenever peoples
are judged by their deeds. The life at Annapo-
lis had served not merely to teach Hobson all the
new devices of the dreadful science he had set out
to learn, but also to develop the forward-looking
planning, eager spirit which was always in him,
and by virtue of which he was American and
democratic to the core. Democracy has its uses
even in a military array. Our highest military
and naval traditions are of enterprise, no less than
obedience to command; of finding the way to victory, no less than marching therein fearlessly.
The incident of his temporary ostracism for re-

porting a classmate, so far from being the extraordinary and sensational martyrdom it has been
painted, was neither unprecedented nor unchar-
acteristic of the place.  He accepted it, as others
have accepted it, simply as a test of his manhood :
such a test as democracies alone afford.  When
his classmates finally offered him fellowship, they
were not conquered revilers of superior merit, but
merely young Americans awakened to the necessity of respecting an honest conviction.  Perhaps
a slight increase of gravity, and the accentuation
of his peculiar formality of speech, may be attributed to the loneliness of his life there ; but the
wound left no ugly scar.  It was not the cause
of his studious habits.  He would have gone to
the head of his class in any event, and would have
been, as he was, a fair mark for such mischievous
girls as delight in harassing a sturdy and untrifling
masculinity.  If heavier chastisement of disappoint-
ment and renunciation was not wanting, it merely
strengthened his devotion to his work, confirmed
his strong religious bent, and armed him completely against all but the last infirmity of noble
minds.  His original and inventive faculty, and
his elaborate study of naval construction, gave
him, no doubt, an especial fitness for his task at

Santiago; but far more essential was the serene self-confidence which his straitened childhood, his harassed boyhood, his chastened young manhood, had helped to build. When the hour of his trial came, it found him no less master of himself than of his ship.

The opportunity was his because he made it. The Spanish fleet, having for a time befooled the board of strategy at Washington, and easily avoided the stronger but slower fleet of Admiral Sampson, had at length taken refuge in the harbor of Santiago. Commodore Schley, hurrying southward from Hampton Roads with the flying squadron, and ascertaining, after some indecision, the whereabouts of the enemy, found the harbor such a rat-hole for narrowness of channel that to enter it seemed to mean the certain loss of the first ship, and this, if sunk in the narrower part of the channel, would effectually block the way for those which followed. Admiral Sampson, arriving soon afterwards, and seeing that the Spanish cruisers had put themselves out of the fighting so long as their exit was barred, at once began to consider if some means could not be found to guard against the only possibility of Cervera's escape: a storm or fog, which might defeat the watchfulness of the Americans. He was no sooner resolved upon the plan than Hobson, who had asked for sea service in view of just such work, was ready with the details of it. It was to sink the *Merrimac*, a huge collier whose defective machinery impaired her usefulness, lengthwise across the channel. Working night and day, he soon had the collier swept clear of her movable cargo, improvised torpedoes placed where their work would be done quickest, and the electric connection arranged. The time she would take to settle, the number of her crew, and the duties of each man, were all minutely calculated and explained. So were the chances of going to the bottom before she could reach her destination. There were the mines, the fire from the forts, her own torpedoes : everything was considered but his own chance of life. Asked about that, he treated the inquiry as irrelevant to the scientific problem he had in hand. It was a question of getting in, not of getting out.

This was not the Latin bravery that dares for the sake of daring. The deed was essentially English, essentially American. It was planned and done in the calm northern mood that belongs to men of clear eyes and quiet speech, and is

commonest among men who pray. Whatever
there was of excitement in it was religious — the
ecstasy of martyrdom. That such a spirit survives among us is more important than that war-
making is become a science, or that the fleet
behind the *Merrimac* was iron clad, or that
modern fortifications, and not merely an ancient
castle, guarded the harbor's mouth.

The spirit was indeed rampant in the fleet. The
signal for volunteers brought an embarrassment of
riches. To choose his companions was the hard-
est part of his making ready. Enough to man a
squadron volunteered, and for these there was less
of fame to win than for the leader. He himself
could not have held fast to his place but for his
share in planning the enterprise and his knowing
best how to carry it out. How dear the enterprise had grown to him since he conceived it was
made clear when it was delayed. All was ready
late in the night of Thursday, the second of June,
and the *Merrimac* set forth ; but the Admiral,
seeing that day was near breaking, sent a torpedo
boat to recall her. It took two orders to bring
her back, and then something happened quite out
of keeping with Hobson's contained and disci-
plined bearing throughout his life. The old

Cromwell stirred in his breast.  Begrimed and
blackened with his work, his face seamed with
lines of sleeplessness and care, his deep eyes no
longer smouldering but aflame, he turned on the
Admiral with such high words as hardly his infe-
riors had ever heard him speak before.  " There
must be no more recalls.  My men have been
keyed up for twenty-four hours, and under a tremendous pressure.  Iron will break at last."
Soothed with good-humored counsel, he waited
impatiently for darkness.

The next night made amends.  It was not dark
or stormy, but the moon was veiled.  The hour
before the dawn was chosen, but many anxious
watchers from the fleet saw the *Merrimac* melt
away into the gloom with the tall figure motionless
on the bridge.  A little launch, meant for the
rescue of any one that might escape both death
and capture, followed behind.  When the collier
came within range of the Spaniard's guns, all left
her but the seven who had been chosen.  Then
for a time the darkness hid her completely, until
at last the signal gun waked the slumbering hell
of the harbor's mouth.  There was an instant roar
of cannonading, and Powell from the launch and
the watchers from the fleet saw the dreadful light

of the firing and even, for a moment, the dark hulk of the *Merrimac* passing onward to her doom. The men in the launch could hear the noise of the torpedoes, but it was not until the swift tropical daybreak came that they could see the masts of the *Merrimac* standing up out of the channel, beyond the point, the Estrella battery, where Hobson had said he would sink her. But the launch waited in vain for the beating of the oars of the returning heroes. In the afternoon, to the Admiral, pacing his quarter-deck, came the messenger of the knightly Cervera to let him know that they lived.

It was not the scientific aspect of this exploit which made so strong an appeal to us all. That was interesting, no doubt ; but the human side of it was, as Carlyle might say, a far greater matter. Its chief interest and value is in its oneness with the historical type of daring made familiar by other English and American seamen whose names were instantly on our lips. Three such names of Americans were brought forward with an especial aptness : Decatur, Somers, and Cushing. The exploits of these three were all directed against a blockaded enemy. Decatur entered the harbor of Tripoli in the ketch *Intrepid*,

boarded the *Philadelphia* under the fire of many
guns, overcame her crew, burnt her, and escaped
without the loss of a man.  Into the same harbor,
shortly after, went Somers, also on the *Intrepid*,
now turned into a mere floating bomb, meaning to
explode her among the huddled ships of the enemy.
But fate was against him.  Before he reached
the inner harbor, the *Intrepid* blew up: whether
from an enemy's shot, or by the act of her
own commander, or from chance, we shall never
know, for none came back to tell.  Cushing,
from the squadron blockading the Carolina coast
in 1864, went up the river Roanoke in a launch,
with seven volunteers, to destroy the Confederate
ram *Albemarle*.  Standing in the prow of his
little vessel, he approached the iron-clad monster
under a rain of bullets.  Finding his way barred
by a boom of logs, he drove the launch full tilt at
the obstacle, slided over it, and then deliberately
swung a torpedo under the ram, sunk her, leaped
into the river, and finally escaped with his life.
Of these four desperate enterprises, including
Hobson's, only one failed completely, and that,
for all we know, may have failed from some cause
that could not have been foreseen.  In the other
three, the reasonableness of daring to the utter-

most was proved by the event. To attempt a
comparison of the four young heroes would be
both useless and vain. Each measured his devotion by the poet's standard : —

> " Give all thou canst; high Heaven neglects the lore
> Of nicely calculated less and more."

But a longer retrospect would be equally appropriate. It might go back to the very beginnings
of our national life : to Paul Jones and the *Bon
Homme Richard;* to Washington himself on the
icy Delaware. We need not stop even there.
Our fancy wanders on to the beginnings of England's sea power, when the might of Spain was not
cabined in blockaded harbors, but flaunted forth
in Armadas. Ralegh or Drake were as good a
peg for a comparison as Cushing or Somers. It
leads us even beyond history, into the legends
and mythology of the North. For what was this
at Santiago but the whole warfare of our race in
little ? What was it the watchers saw from the fleet
but the immemorial ship that disappears into the
unknown ? What, but the young Siegfried enter-
ing the cave of the dragon ? What, but Arthur
passing into the dying day ? To peer into the
soul of this high-fortuned youth is to feel the

higher mood of the race, in which all the wonders of our past have been wrought out. It is to lean upon the strength which shall fight the battles of this Republic so long as it survives and battles are to fight.

# VI.  SHIFTING THE WHITE
##   MAN'S  BURDEN

# VI

## SHIFTING THE WHITE MAN'S BURDEN

Is Mason and Dixon's line still a boundary line? That question must come into many men's minds the day after a presidential election, when it appears that the South has gone one way and practically all the rest of the country another. We may, in fact, put the matter more strongly still, and say that the South votes on one question and the rest of the country on another, or others. Certainly, there is a very real sense in which the historic line does still separate those Americans who can, from those who apparently cannot, enjoy their political birthright to the full.

That such is the case, and that Southerners themselves realize the situation as they have not heretofore, has been borne in upon me by much free talk with men of all classes from the Potomac to the Rio Grande: with legislators and judges, with the chairmen of state committees, with congressmen and senators, with clergymen and lawyers and business men, and with the man on the street corner. The sense of it, the restiveness under it, which all intelligent and thoughtful Southerners display, is particularly striking in men of the old ruling class. One such man, who as a boy served in the Confederate army, who as a young man led in the struggle against the carpet-baggers, who for years has belonged to the comparatively small group which controls the Democratic party machinery of his state, and who now holds a high state office, confessed to me with genuine sadness in his voice that he did not expect to live long enough to vote as he believes on national questions. It was his prayer that his sons might some day have a privilege denied to him. This feeling, even before men were willing to express it, began to have its effects in Southern politics. And it is in part responsible for what is doing now.

The main thing doing now is something which began ten years ago in Mississippi and which in a few years, unless all signs fail, will have worked itself out in every state where the blacks are nearly so numerous as the whites. Mississippi, by a constitutional amendment passed in 1890, legalized that disfranchisement of the bulk of her negro citizens which was accomplished fact already, and had been so for years. South Carolina, in 1895, by an amendment somewhat different from Mississippi's, did practically the same thing. Louisiana followed in 1897, and North Carolina in 1900. Virginia and Alabama have fallen into line. Even Maryland has taken up the plan.

What is the conviction or impulse that started the movement? What is the true character of the change itself? Is there any good reason to regard it as a solution, or as in any wise leading up to the solution, of the problem which we have so long debated and compromised and fought over? Is it another crime, another blunder sure to prove as disastrous as a crime, or are we on the right track at last?

An increasing number, but still far too small a number of Southerners, are asking these things of themselves and their fellows with a deep and painful sense of responsibility. Northern men are asking them, too, but in no such imperious tones as they formerly used. The feeling of responsibility seems, in fact, to have strengthened in the men of the South as the feeling of helpless disapproval has taken hold of Northern

men.  Congress, by refusing to take the disfranchisement movement into account in passing the
reapportionment act of 1901, practically gave the
Southerners a free hand for the time being ; and
the faintness of the protest from the North exhibits a state of public opinion there utterly
without parallel in recent history.  Every attempt
from the outside to fix the relations between
black men and white men in the South has
either been completely negatived or has had results wholly unlike those it aimed at.  So nowadays, though the Northern philanthropist still
gives money to educational and other charitable
enterprises to help the blacks, and though the
Northern reformer still denounces, the responsible public men of the North are disinclined
to interfere.

We cannot understand what the Southerners
are doing unless we remind ourselves that the
negro question is only one side, and not the
most important side, of the Southern question.
The main thing is not what to do for the negro,
but what to do for the white man living among
negroes.  That, certainly, is the Southerners'
point of view, and it is not unreasonable.  More
numerous, and of a race whose capacity for civili-

zation and for self-government is amply proved, why should they be held of less account than the representatives of a race which has never, unaided, shown itself capable either of civilization or of self-government? Shall we spend all our thought on strengthening the weak, and have no care of the strong?[1]

Depressing as the Southern negro is to the thoughtful traveller, the illiterate Southern white man is more depressing still. On many a lonely highway they pass each other; on many a village street corner they mutely reproach each other; sometimes, face to face in public conveyances, they stare at each other in helpless antagonism, felt, perhaps, but not understood. To overcome that antagonism, to save both together, would be an achievement sufficient to make a man's name illustrious forever with Lincoln's. To lift up one without the other is itself no mean enterprise. The disfranchisement movement, now completing with constitutional conventions what the Ku Klux began, appears on

[1] The comparison with the Philippine situation, attempted during the campaign of 1901, was far fetched. The weaker race is here the alien, however involuntary its original intrusion; the disturbing element in the population, not the main body of the people.

the surface to be an attempt merely to strike down one politically, leaving the other as he was before.

It is a mistaken view of the history of slavery in America which represents that institution as battling only against the public opinion of the outside world, and finally yielding only because it was attacked from without. It was the internal weakness of the slave system — its economic, political, intellectual, and moral unfitness to survive — that brought it into collision with the forces that destroyed it. From the beginning, it had within it the seeds of death. To understand its downfall, we must study the decay within, and not merely the hostility without. And so, too, of the race question to-day. The only fruitful study of it is from the inside; and such a study will be inconclusive unless it take into account things which cannot be set down in figures or arrayed in tables and diagrams. We may exhibit with figures the material progress both races have made since the whites regained control in the seventies. The state of education also has been frequently set forth with reasonable clearness. As to the political situation, we have abundance of statistics showing that, vol-

untarily or involuntarily, the negroes forego their
citizenly rights wherever, by reason of their
numbers, they might control. These things,
however, help us little unless we realize how
they are based in the human nature of both
races and how they react upon both.

The suppression of negro votes, whether by violence, intimidation, or mere trickery, has not been
common to the whole South. It has been confined to portions of certain states—particularly
the "Black Belt" of the Cotton states, the richer
agricultural regions in other states, and the cities
generally. These, however, are the very quarters
in which the political control of the South was
lodged before the Civil War, partly because they
profited most by the constitutional provision allow-
ing representation to three-fifths of the slaves,
partly because they were inhabited by the most
intelligent and masterful Southerners of those
days. It was the survivors of that class who led
the way out of bondage after reconstruction, and
once more gained for themselves the foremost
places in Southern society. Their leadership,
readily accepted at the time, was in large measure
justified by the ability and fidelity they displayed
in party conventions and committees and in pub-

lic office. Practising the most rigid economy, they brought the finances of the state governments, exploited as they had been by the carpet-baggers, into a surprisingly good condition, and they did the like for the counties and the towns. So intimately were politics at that time related to the welfare of individuals and families, so necessary was honesty and ability in office, that the strongest sort of public sentiment demanded the putting forward of good men, and there was little intriguing among the whites. For some years, in fact, the state and local governments were administered as capably and honestly as, for the most part, they had been administered before the war; and that is saying much.

But the wrong at the bottom of the system, like the wrong in slavery, began very soon to work itself out. The carpet-bagger disappeared. The negroes made less and less effort to get a share of power, contenting themselves perforce with such morsels of Federal patronage as were thrown to them when their white leaders were compensated for helping to nominate successful candidates in Republican national conventions. The Republican party in the South broke into factions and ceased to be really dangerous except in spots.

The old ruling class, though shorn of its wealth, and though its ascendency in national politics was gone forever, was just as strongly intrenched in power at home as it was in 1860. Moreover, its power was as clearly bottomed on the freedman as it had ever been bottomed on the slave. The "black" counties, represented in legislatures and party conventions according to an apportionment based on the theory that negroes were voters, had an undue ascendency over the "white" counties, just as they had before the war. This ascendency was in fact heightened by the granting of representation to two-fifths of the negroes, not counted under slavery.

Two consequences of these conditions led directly to the clamor for disfranchisement. One was the loss of respect for the ballot-box among the whites who profited most by the suppression of negro votes, and the inevitable extension of unfair practices into their own party primaries and conventions. The other was the discontent of white men not of the ruling class, stimulated and enlarged by the wider discontent of the farming class throughout the country. The antagonism of the white counties to the black counties had run through the political history of the South from the beginning. The granger movement, culminating in South Carolina in the victory of Tillman, when the new men actually got control of the dominant party, and elsewhere in the rise of a party which, whatever names it took in different states, was always the party of discontent with the existing order, was a new development, and its peculiar importance in the South has never been properly emphasized.

In other parts of the country, this movement was distinctly a protest against industrial conditions, and against the "money power" in particular. In the South also it had, at first, somewhat of that character; but very soon it developed there into an uprising, rather political than social, against the groups of men who controlled the Democratic machines, and thereby controlled the entire political life, of the several states. It became a fight of the outs against the ins. The outs were made up chiefly of small farmers in the richer agricultural regions, up to that time ordinarily inclined to follow the lawyers and planters, and the bulk of the citizens of the upland regions, in which most of the "white" counties lay. The ins consisted of the office-holding class, of conservatives who dreaded any division among the whites as the chief danger to society, and in general of such as found in the existing order the means of welfare or a stay to their pride.

In South Carolina, where the outs won by getting possession of the machine, the retirement of such men as Hampton and Butler, to make way for Tillman and Irby, marked a revolution in the internal politics of the little state deeper than the changes of 1776 and 1860. In North Carolina, somewhat later, by combining with the Republicans, the party of discontent overthrew the Democratic machine at the polls. That victory resulted in such misgovernment, particularly in counties and towns, that North Carolina, formerly less inclined to discriminate against negro voters than other Southern states, has gone even farther than South Carolina dared to go in the direction of disfranchisement. In the other states, the uprising against the old leaders was either defeated or compromised with, and the chief of the means employed to defeat it was the negro vote in those counties where negroes were most numerous. The contest revealed clearly the basis of the power of the ruling class; it threw into clearer light than ever before the political antagonism between the "white" and "black" counties;

and it also made clear the impossibility of having one code of political morality in dealing with negroes and another code in dealing with white men.

The negroes had taken but little part in the controversy, but their votes, whether cast or not, had been of the utmost importance. The contention that the whites must not divide lest the blacks get into power lost much of its force, for the whites had divided and the negroes had not come into power. Nevertheless, the feeling against negro suffrage was heightened rather than diminished, for it was seen that negro votes, even though they were not cast, or were counted to suit the Democratic managers, were still an obstacle to the popular will. If the actual exercise of the suffrage by negroes threatened property and order, the suppression of their votes brought about conditions destructive of equality among the whites. In other words, whether exercised or not, the legal right of the negro to vote was seen to be a stumbling-block in the way of democracy.

The discontent of thoughtful and high-minded citizens with conditions which seemed to necessitate deception and fraud was already manifest. There was a marked tendency among such men

to withdraw from active party work, either volun-
tarily or because less squeamish aspirants for
leadership had, in the nature of things, an advantage over them. This discontent, however,
was not alone adequate to bring about a change.
It needed to be reinforced by the discontent of
the less thoughtful but far larger class of outs
who made up the bulk of the Tillman party in
South Carolina and the Kolb party in Alabama,
and who, in every state, if not conciliated, drifted
for the most part into populism.

Moreover, as I have said, Southerners are restive
under the restraints which keep them from enter-
ing actively and fearlessly into the larger political
life of the Republic. Americanism is growing in
the South. Pride in the flag, pride in the prosperity and prestige of the United States, is surely
heightening. Industrial development has brought
many regions, hitherto remote and separate, into
close business relations with the North. Merchants
and bankers are constantly visiting New York and
other eastern cities. Metropolitan newspapers are
read everywhere. Women's clubs are active in
every large town. The plantation no longer sets
the standard of social usage and intellectual life.
The whole South is too much alive to outer things,

too cognizant of a civilization ampler than its own, not to feel keenly the limitations upon its participation in national political contests. Its political solidarity, once a source of pride, is now seldom vaunted; oftener, it is explained and apologized for. The negro is, of course, the sole explanation, the sole apology. To get rid of him politically, and to do it by law, once for all, is the only remedy proposed.

But whenever there is discussion of specific plans the illiterate white man is bound to come in. Mississippi provides for him by permitting the registrars to decide that he understands the state constitution and the negro does not. The Supreme Court of the United States has sustained that provision, but obviously it merely transfers the task of suppressing negro votes from the inspectors at the polls to the registrars of voters. A division among the whites might still, at any time, lead to the registering of negroes. The change has not perceptibly bettered Mississippi's politics, and there was no good reason to believe it would. North Carolina and Louisiana provide for the illiterate white by admitting him to registration if he or his ancestors could vote before the Reconstruction Acts were passed. The consti-

tutionality of this plan has not yet been passed
upon. South Carolina, of the four states which
have already acted, seems to have made the least
elaborate provision for him. As yet, however,
no Southern state has adopted a simple educational
qualification for the suffrage, and in none of the
states which are still to act is there any probabil-
ity that such a qualification will be fixed. Unquestionably, there is a strong preference for that
straightforward course among thoughtful Southerners, but the practical politicians fight shy of
it, contending openly that illiteracy frequently
does not imply unfitness for citizenship, and con-
fessing privately that the fate of the plan, if
submitted to popular vote, would be extremely
doubtful. Another plan is to debar negroes from
public office by constitutional enactment, on the
theory that office-holding is not one of the rights
secured to them by the Fourteenth Amendment.
One eminent Southern public man, after long
study of the question, can find no solution of it
save in the repeal of the Fifteenth Amendment
and the absolute denial to the negro, as a negro,
of the right to vote. A justice of a Southern
Supreme Court so far coincides with him as to
declare that no remedy will be effective which

simply transfers fraud from the ballot box to the statute book.

Such is the case in which Southern white men find themselves, and such the latest movement looking toward betterment. Confessedly, it is not a movement to help the negro. Yet its advocates maintain that its effects on the negro, incidental though they be, will prove beneficial rather than the reverse. What good, they ask, has the negro ever got from participation in politics, even in those regions where his vote is counted? A few exceptional negroes, like Bruce and Douglas, have shown themselves fit to play a part in public affairs, but the great majority of negro politicians are declared, by such representatives of their own race as Booker T. Washington and William H. Councill, to be doing more harm than good. To get the negro out of politics and into remunerative work, so these men say, is one of the first steps toward true progress.

But while men like Washington do not cry out against the denial of the ballot to the illiterate and unintelligent mass of their fellows, they do protest against the methods by which it has been accomplished in defiance of law and the plans tried or proposed for legalizing it. Granting that a large

proportion, perhaps a majority, of the negroes are
unfit for office and unready for the suffrage,
they nevertheless object to the exclusion of unfit
negroes by any test or before any tribunal
which will not similarly exclude unfit white men.
In effect, the best representatives of both races
are at one on the question of what should be
done. But the main thing is, what can be done,
what will be done.

The tribunal, and not the law, is the real difficulty. The rulers of Southern states and counties
and towns do at the present time, whenever they
deem it necessary, deny to negroes the political
power which the law confers upon them. That
course is in accord with the public sentiment of
the communities in which it is followed. The
practices thus established, the habit of mind thus
contracted, will not disappear at once with the
conditions in which they originated. When a
disease has made a certain progress, it cannot be
cured merely by removing the cause. Negro
suffrage has vitiated the political morality of the
South, but it does not follow that to disfranchise
the bulk of the negroes is to purify politics. How
to get tribunals which will treat negroes and
white men alike is a problem not yet solved, and

it will not be solved until public opinion shall demand that they be treated alike.

The disfranchisement movement, then, is very far from being a solution of the race question in its political phase. It does not leave the negro in a position which either those who believe in his capacity for development or those who are governed entirely by the prejudice against him will be content to regard as permanent. The law will discriminate against him so far as the law-makers dare, and registration boards will be governed by the same public sentiment which now justifies the practices of inspectors at the polls. He will have the same shadowy political equality which he now has, and which to some minds seems worse for him, as it is doubtless worse for the whites, than if the Fourteenth and Fifteenth Amendments were repealed and his inequality plainly declared by law. As to the whites, the temptation to questionable practices, or rather to practices unquestionably bad, will be diminished, but not entirely removed. They will be freer to divide among themselves, but there is little prospect of their immediately abandoning that provincial and defensive attitude toward their country which so oppresses their leading minds.

On the whole, however, the movement is progressive rather than reactionary. It is a recognition of actual conditions, an envisagement of facts hitherto never frankly acknowledged. It is an attempt, half hearted, perhaps, but not wholly dishonest, to bring the political life of the South into accord with the written law by changing the law. It will tend, therefore, to heighten the respect for the law. It is, moreover, the work of the better class of politicians, acting in obedience to public sentiment. One is favorably impressed with it if one considers only who are in favor of it and who are against it. Whether or not it is a victory for good government, it seems to be, in the main, a victory for good men.

But the problem is of free government rather than of good government, and it cannot be separated from the greater problem of which it is a part. The disfranchisement movement does not aim to alter the general attitude of the two races toward each other; and so long as that attitude remains the same, Southern politics will remain unlike the politics of the North. The trouble is not in laws and institutions; it is in men. It is not in the organization of the body politic, but in its composition. When de Tocqueville declared that he could explain every one of the differences between the North and South by the institution of slavery, he overstated the importance of the institution. He magnified the evil of slavery, and neglected the slave.

When due account is taken of all the blunders we have made in dealing with the negro, — and they have been many, — of all the crimes we have committed against him, — and they have been flagrant, — it remains true that not they, but he himself, by his mere presence here, is the main source of our present-day perplexities. The political isolation of the South, like its separateness in other respects, is due to the negro, and to the inevitable effects on white men of living among negroes. It is thirty-five years since the slaves were freed, but the shadow of Africa still rests upon the land.

At the rear of a shop in a thriving city in the newly developed mineral region of Alabama I saw, at midday, a burly negro stretched on his back, eyes shut, mouth open, wrapt in peaceful slumber. On the street corner outside stood a white countryman, awake but utterly idle, a vague, childlike inquiry in his face, watching whatsoever passed on the other side of the street. What passed was characteristic of the New South; but the sleeping negro, the listless poor white, burdened my mind in spite of the stir of business about them, and the smoke of furnaces and factories, and the tooting of engines in the distance. Not even material progress and prosperity, welcome and creditable as they are, can satisfy us concerning the civilization in which those two figures keep their places.

But there are genuinely hopeful signs: signs of progress in the two directions in which alone true and lasting betterment can reasonably be hoped for. Hampton and Tuskegee on the one hand, the Montgomery conferences on the other, are infinitely more encouraging than anything doing or anything that can possibly be done at Washington or in state legislatures or in constitutional conventions. For democracy rests on the sense, if not the reality, of equality among men. Communities made up of races so disposed toward each other as the Southern whites and blacks now are cannot live up to democratic standards, no matter what their laws may be. To alter the white man's attitude toward the negro, to rid the negro of those characteristics which humanly necessitate, although they may not justify, the white man's attitude toward him — these are the two things that must be done.

The difficulty of these two tasks is not to be underestimated, — not even in view of the transcendent importance, the necessity, of getting them done. As to the negro, it will not be enough if, imitative above all things, he fashion his life outwardly after the white man's. He must be inwardly remade. He must, in his own mind, erect himself into the full stature of the manhood that beats down his own. As to the white man, he must unlearn the lesson of his own imperious, masterful dominance. He must, somehow, learn to believe that there is that in the negro which the negro's habit of servility belies. He must obey that higher law which still, above all statutes and constitutions, impels with an obligation which no written law can ever make compelling. The obligation is to forbearance, to gentleness, to sympathy; to the entire fairness which shall not take account of rights; to the brotherhood which alone can make of equality before the law anything but the hideous mockery it is to-day.

Is either of those tasks humanly possible? Which is the more hopeful? Which the more important? Both, clearly, are educational. Education of some sort is the only device yet suggested to accomplish either.

The common belief is that of the two the task of changing the negroes by education is the more hopeful, since there is among them a greater density of ignorance, and so the possibility of a greater progress. It is also held to be the more important, on the theory that it alone will make possible a different attitude of the whites toward the blacks. Tuskegee and Hampton are therefore regarded as the best of all the agencies at work.

They are, indeed, wholly admirable; they are infinitely deserving. Nevertheless, I am drawn to the conviction that the other of the two tasks is, on the whole, the more hopeful, the more practical, the more important. I feel sure it is freer from any shadow of a doubt that it will be vain, even if it be accomplished. We know, and know precisely, what there is to gain by educating white men of English stocks. We do not know precisely how much there is to gain by educating a large negro population. I am speaking now of the immediate gain, without reference to the race problem. We know farther, as to the race problem itself, that it is vastly less perplexing when educated white men deal with negroes, whether educated or illiterate, than when ignorant white men deal with negroes of either class. Substitute for the hundreds of thousands of Southern whites who cannot read, and the greater numbers whose ability to read and write is the sum total of their culture, an equal body of educated whites, correspondingly more thrifty, cleanly, aspiring, reasonable, intelligent, — and we know that education means these things with men of English stocks, — and there is not one of us who doubts that the situation will be immeasurably bettered. Leave the whites as they are, and educate the negroes, and no candid mind will be free from doubts and fears of the result. To educate both races up to the limit of their capacities is, of course, the complete ideal. To educate the whites is the safest, the easiest, the wisest first step to take.

Facing back over Southern history is not cheering. Facing forward is trying to the stoutest-hearted optimism. The fallacy in most of our debating is, in fact, the fallacy of wilful optimism. We have constantly assumed that there was a solution of each problem as it presented itself, a clearly right thing to do, which could also be done. There is still no occasion to despair. But we must take up every new plan with the chastening knowledge that most of our devices have failed; that nothing which can be quickly accomplished will go deep enough to last; that no sudden illumination will ever come, nor any swift breaking of the clouds shed sunlight on our shadowed land. Africa still mocks America from her jungles. "Still," she jeers, "with the dense darkness of my ignorance, I confound your enlightenment. Still, with my sloth, I weigh down the arms of your industry. Still, with my supineness, I hang upon the wings of your aspiration. And in the very heart of your imperial young republic I have planted, sure and deep, the misery of this ancient curse I bear."